ENERGETIC AWAKENING

LIVING A GUIDED LIFE

ANNMARIE L. EARLY
ANNIE L. BROWNING

Copyright © 2021 by Annmarie L. Early and Annie L. Browning

All rights reserved.

No part of this book may be reproduced in any form or by any electronic or mechanical means, including information storage and retrieval systems, without written permission from the author, except for the use of brief quotations in a book review.

Cover and Interior Designs by Homestead Publishing Co.

CONTENTS

Introduction	v
1. THE ENERGETICS OF AWAKENING	1
Positioning	3
Inhabiting Your Sacred Centers	3
Positioning Dimensionally	7
Essence and Vibrational Energies	8
Following the Path of Energetic Awakening	10
Energetic Experiencing	13
2. SPARKING AND CRACKING	16
Unearthing Soul Seeds	17
Sparking	22
Cracking	27
Calling You Home	31
Energetic Experiencing	31
3. MISMATCHING AND MISSTEPS	34
Making Messes	36
Embracing What No Longer Fits	42
Energetic Experiencing	44
4. VACILLATING VOICES	46
Recognizing the Voice of Your YOU	48
Knowing the Voice of the Soul	50
Yielding	51
Living Within Yieldedness	56
Loving the Ego	57
Thinning of Your *You*	59
Energetic Experiencing	60
5. NAVIGATING BETWEEN WORLDS	63
Walking Between Worlds	64
Following Life's Streams	65
Inhabiting the Depths	71

Between Two Worlds	75
Energetic Experiencing	78
6. RISING WORLDS THAT MEET YOU	**81**
A New Location Within	82
Withinness	84
Something From No-Thing	86
Rising Worlds	88
Receiving Guidance From Your Soul	91
Guidance	105
Energetic Experiencing	108
7. FALLING INTO UNDOING	**111**
THRESHOLD CROSSING	112
Led By Your Soul	113
Wandering in the Wilderness	115
Falling Away of Identity	116
Where Did My Mind Go?	117
Companioning	119
Do Not Be Afraid	120
Energetic Experiencing	121
8. ENTERING A NEW WORLD	**124**
Awakening Landscapes	125
Dimensional Positioning: The 5 R's	128
Living Life Awake	136
Energetic Experiencing	137
9. LIVING A GUIDED LIFE	**140**
A New Paradigm	141
The New World: Essence and Vibration in Action	144
Awakening the World	149
Epilogue	152
About the Authors	155

INTRODUCTION

We invite you to join us on a journey home to the truth of what you are. This invitation does not come from us. It is a larger energy that is moving through our world. We are simply the voice that speaks the words for your ears to hear. The words that you will read in this book are a bell ringing, calling you back—they speak directly to you about who and what you are. You do not need to be special to hear the ringing. You do not need to have attained some level of spiritual mastery to heed the call. It doesn't matter where you live or what your circumstances are. The bell that rings, rings for you.

We happen to live in a time on this planet where the world is moving and shaking, reorienting the very ground beneath our feet. It is experienced by many as disorienting, and it is perceived as a falling apart or a time of disintegration. And, in many ways this describes exactly what is happening—though it is different from what you might expect. All of this movement that you feel around you is purposeful. It is energetic. Illusion is collapsing and there is a rising in our midst that is calling to each one of us to live more fully from the truth of what we are. To learn to follow what is happening in the larger world we have to learn how to track the energy, not the circumstances of what is happening. We are beckoned through this energetic process to alter our life's course so that we, as a people, do not run our ship aground. It is time to wake up to what we are and to begin living from a more soulful place in every aspect of our lived experience.

This is energetic awakening. We, you, are called to live more awake in every aspect of our life. It is energetic in that it is primarily sparked through intuitive process and it is all encompassing. No aspect of life is untouched. There is nothing unwelcome and you are perched exactly where you need to be to say yes to the sparking in your soul. You need not be special or set apart in any way. Energetic awakening is for everyone, now, for that is what awakening is most essentially about.

What we offer to you in this book is a way to actively engage the energy of awakening. You are guided through energetic awakening movements that naturally move you throughout the process—ones that teach you how to track energy movements that carry you into awakening within the ordinary aspects of your life. These movements can be applied within your current faith perspective and they can offer you orienting markers if you do not have a spirituality that you adhere to. The movements are universal and without the need for a belief system. They are as natural as your breath.

As you learn to follow the movement of energetic awakening you will wake up. It is simply what happens when you learn to follow the movements of energy that guide you. For, what the world needs now is a form of awakening that changes how we live and where we live from. It requires that the world keep ticking while mothers and business people, students and grandfathers, children and those dying learn to live from a different place within every moment of every day. The call to live awake is universal and it is for you. It is energetic and it will carry you. It's time to wake up.

The Movements of Energetic Awakening

One of the hallmarks of energetic awakening movement is simplicity. Spirituality has become far too complicated with too many steps and complex required practices. It has stayed in the mind and of the mind. We are in a time of radical regeneration where our mental systems are being broken down brick by brick. Our tendency when something is falling down is to build back up what is broken. We do this in the world through service and action and we do this in our spirituality as well. We fill the emptied out space with good ideas for change and more of what is wanted in our practices and prayers.

Energetic Awakening is different—it follows the naturally present energies in our world that invite us to live anew. It does not create a new system. The movement of energetic awakening is a deep withinness that supports the natural process of dismantling and the quiet of stillness that opens into something more that awaits us. Energetic awakening allows what is unnecessary to fall away. It orients you to the natural movements of awakened living, but it does not describe them to you and ask you to find them. Rather, energetic awakening leads you into energies that carry you, giving you orienting markers along that way that help you to let go just a little bit more and follow the larger movements in our world.

The pathway of energetic awakening is a descending spiral that opens into a more soulful way to live. The spiral is one of descent that moves you downward and deeper in, grounding you more fully in this world, while positioning you more soulfully within your true center. The energetic awakening process is on a spiral that descends rather than on an ascending ladder for a very important reason—it is one of release and yielding rather than a building up and transcendence of. Anything that ascends tends to build up more of something, ungrounding, and potentially bypassing the necessary process of release. The energetic awakening descent naturally lets go of and releases, allowing what is extraneous and of illusion to fall away.

It is a spiral because the path never ends. You deepen your awareness and open more and more to the truth of what you are expanding into dimensional spaces of infinite possibility, but the road is never complete. And it is a path of descent known more for what isn't there than what is. Energetic awakening is a process of release and letting go. As you shed the layers of what you thought you were, you open to your truth of what lies in the unseen spaces around you and this allows you to live more fully from the soul. That is the process of Energetic Awakening.

Tracking Energy

Throughout this process you learn to track the energy of awakening. Awakening is a movement, not a static thing to achieve—that is the construction of the mind and what keeps awakening mental. Energetic awakening requires an inward attention to the vacillations of energy—how they open and when they collapse, when to follow a movement through to completion and when the process settles, the difference between the quiet of the mind and being within stillness where once you rest here a space opens around you. The key is learning to be fully within—noticing when you are even slightly outside of an experience and how that alters movement—and how to follow from this space.

Awakening is a process that continually moves as you track essence and vibration energies in your life and in the world. Your developing ability to follow energetic processes is what deepens you into your awakening. The energetic spaces within and around are alive and present. Over time, you will learn to not only track, but be in relationship with these energies in a living, reciprocal conversation. You will enter the space of manifestation—bringing forth what you most want in your life—where your sense-abilities will heighten and expand.

Loving the *You*

For all of the undoing and reorienting that awakening involves, energetic awakening is a gentle process that allows all of us to remain in our lives with access to every part of our embodied existence. We focus on positioning rather than eradicating our unwanted parts or bringing force to the change process in order for something to die. Rather, we recognize the place of the egoic mind (what we will refer to as your *You*) and the importance of your *You* in your everyday functioning. Without access to any ego (mind) it is very difficult to get your bills paid and your kids to school on time. We honor the place of your *You* (ego) and we provide practical support for its quieting, allowing it to come forward at the right times and places. Instead of overcoming the *You* we befriend it as we live more fully from a different set point within—the place of the soul.

Falling into Undoing

And, finally, energetic awakening requires a season of radical release. Many people awaken in the mind and allow their life to hum along as it always has. Energetic awakening sees the undoing of the *You* as a central aspect to full, embodied awakened living. Without the process of falling away, there is simply too much stuff within each one of us that clutters and takes up space. Falling into undoing removes the clutter allowing energy to flow unimpeded.

We have no idea when or how undoing will happen for you, but we can promise you that it will, for not one of us gets to keep our identity intact. There is a sifting and sorting that the process of energetic awakening demands and the contents of your life will be reordered. The orienting markers along the way will help you to release your grip and follow the movement that carries you. As you learn to move with these natural rhythms of release, you will expand into a way of being within life that opens you into everything.

Returning Home

Energetic awakening is for everyone for it is a return home to the truth of what we really are. The call is energetic for the movement, not the thoughts about what we think and believe, are what will carry you home. Each step you take, each orienting marker that you release into, clears more space for the essence and vibration of what you are to come forward in your life and in the world. The movement is natural. The movement is the energetic foundation of this world.

For we are all called to return to a truth about existence that transcends the conception and creation of the mind. No longer can we live within a paradigm that supports living, working, and dying as the package that holds our incarnational existence. We are beings of light, expressions of that which is the divine source from which we come and our life, no matter how or where we are living it, has a purpose that extends beyond the reaches of time. We are all connected in the large expanse that holds all form and creation and it is that essential knowing that will change the landscape of the world that we live in, one spark at a time.

How you engage with this book is more important than any understanding you might gain by reading it. You are participating in an energetic process that will open and move you simply by engaging in it. This may not make a lot of sense at first and your mind may not understand what we are saying. Actually, it is better if it doesn't. Learning to follow awakening processes from within your emerging experience is the key. By tracking these unfolding movements that are rising from within, you will open into a space that will become your guide and an alive way of knowing.

But, enough of that for now, for the journey is just beginning. You need only take the first step. Turn the page and be led forward to meet your life in a completely new way that will change everything about the life you have lived so far.

1

THE ENERGETICS OF AWAKENING

Imagine yourself in medieval England, a commoner, and a woman. You are unable to read or write and you have no formal education. You are the mother of fourteen children and you begin to have mystical experiences that change your life forever.

Margery Kempe lived in Norfolk, England in the 14th century and she began to have visions after the birth of her first child. Her visions included visitations from Jesus and Mary, a vivid account of standing at the foot of the cross during Jesus's crucifixion and they were often accompanied by loud weeping and wailing. Margery was widely condemned for these visions and she faced multiple charges of heresy throughout her life. She proclaimed that she was an intercessor and she preached these teachings making claims and demonstrations of emotion that were seen as only acceptable for those in the priesthood, those "close to God."

Her legacy includes an autobiography that was lost for centuries penned by scribes she commissioned to write down her story. She unabashedly details her path of knowing God even in the face of outward condemnation. She weaves together her experiences of raising children, brewing and milling grain, and making pilgrimages throughout Europe where she details her colorful and vivid conversations with Jesus. Margery's life has many aspects that are ordinary for a woman of her time and yet her life is anything but mundane. Her vantage point in life is unique— unorthodox, especially for a woman— and yet she speaks and lives from this inspired place. Margery sees through her circumstances, her place and position, into something larger that is calling her. She allows this message to ring forward for our ears to hear through her writings and she points us toward the power of awakening.

Have you ever known something even though you don't have anything tangible to support your knowing? It's like looking at one of those geometric pictures at a distance. As you move closer and relax your vision, what was fuzzy just a moment ago suddenly changes and you see a boat floating at sea. Once you see it you know what the picture is—it's simply there whether you zoom out or in. It's the same process with energetic awakening. You walk the path of awakening using an inner tracking of energy that may feel like nothing at first. Over time, as you sink further into your experiencing, you learn to tune in and then follow the movement of energetic awakening.

The key is the movement out of the mind and into a wiser place within that is waiting for you. Many people have had mental awakenings—one's where they understand distinct consciousness shifts. They experience a clarity of insight and understanding that is compelling, but it doesn't seem to change much in their everyday life. Energetic Awakening is different. In the process of energetic awakening, you enter a positioning that moves you into a fullness where rather than knowing a difference in one moment of illumination, a deeper knowingness opens over time and changes everything about how you experience your life. What you can't see in the moment you can look back on realizing how far you have traveled. How you experience and live in the world— and within yourself— shifts.

Positioning

The energetic awakening process doesn't require you to move to a mountain top or to leave the life that you are living. Rather, from within what is most simple and ordinary in your everyday life you begin to live from a different place —a different position— that reorients you to your inner world and the larger world around you. Where you live— your house, the city you live in— may not change, but where you live *from* does.

We refer to this process as coming home to the truth of what you are. This return involves a process of centering within where you begin to access both the wise voice of your soul and the wisdom of the unseen spaces around you. You are not finding anything new. Rather, you are returning to something essential... You are coming home by positioning yourself in your center.

There are two kinds of centering that we will introduce. One is learning to center within—what we refer to as putting yourself in your home base—and the other is centering dimensionally in a larger surround that opens up when you awaken. We will begin with how to return to center within and offer pointers for how to begin to track the energetic processes from within that space.

Inhabiting Your Sacred Centers

There are positions that help in energetic awakening because they orient us in a place for receiving. There are whole traditions that support this process. Keep these practices if they work for you. Simply add our descriptions and place them within your own way of positioning yourself as we walk forward from here. Our goal is to offer simple steps that unfold naturally and over time become your orienting set point to return to.

We believe that this is important because we have found in our own lives and in our work with others that there are practices that help and practices that get in the way and stop the movement we are trying to embody. It can be different for every person and so what is right for you may not work for me, no matter how hard I try.

For example, there are extensive traditions around meditation. Meditation can be the pathway for positioning you right where you need to be, still and open from within. In our experience, we know both the meditation that relaxes us into and the meditation that becomes the stumbling block that trips and bars the passageway. You might know the difference yourself. You try to sit and meditate and all that happens is more thoughts that you try to distance from or quiet. They get louder and louder until the monkey is ruling your monkey mind. Over time, the mind might quiet, but it also may become effort and suffering. And for others, meditation is the smooth pathway of release that places you just where you need to open. Allow yourself to be wherever you are and to become curious and open about what will support you moving forward from here.

We offer **Aligning** and **Awareness** as two simple practices for positioning yourself within your centers that help to ready you for release and deepen your ability to listen and receive, even as you are reading through this book.

Aligning

Alignment is the ability to come to your Sacred Centers and position yourself there to be ready to receive. The first step of aligning is to realize that you are more than your body. You have an energy field that extends around your skin that is a 360-degree-egg-shaped encasing that reaches about three to four feet out. Your energy field does many things, but for our purposes you will need to be inside of your energy sphere to center. If there are parts of you scattered about or connected to other things or people you are not fully in your energy sphere.

Simply bring your awareness to your energy field and imagine collecting all of you into it, including feelings or sensations that at first might be uncomfortable. Release anyone or any circumstance that might draw you away and simply feel yourself inside of your energy field, imagining light particles collecting and moving inward toward your center.

Your Sacred Heart Center is in the middle of your chest and you will bring all of you in there to that centering position. Place yourself in your Sacred Heart Center—not trying to do it—simply following the action of positioning and allowing awareness to guide you. You can put a hand on your heart center to help you feel the tangibility of this position. This positioning is a home base to return to that is powerful and has a quality of holding presence even while circumstances might swirl about you.

There is also a Sacred Wisdom Center around your navel that has wise information for you. When you bring your awareness there while simultaneously staying in your Sacred Heart Center, you are in a more aligned position within. Even if you don't notice anything at first, this positioning will help you to live centered and over time it will become the place that you go to as your home base to open to a form of listening that will rise within you. Throughout your practice, you may notice nothing or lots of something. It really doesn't matter. Allow the position of alignment to guide you and open you.

Expanding Awareness

While you read this book, we encourage you to try positioning yourself within your Sacred Centers to support you in expanding your awareness to receive what you are meant to hear, know, sense and open to as you are reading the written words on the page.

Awareness expands from within a position of alignment where you sink into the stillness within—a space that we refer to as the void. The void may sound like nothing, but it is an alive something from which listening rises. The mystery is that awareness—the wise knowing within—comes not from your efforting, but by allowing the stillness to be your starting place. From here, you begin to listen to what rises within and around you. We call this your divine *guidance* and it rises from the subtle, mystical, and natural realms informing you in soulful steps forward.

We encourage you to practice alignment and expanding awareness because we believe there is something larger leading in the process—we are being led to write about awakening in a particular way and you also will be led to hear, receive, and express your own voice from within this experiencing. In order for these words to become alive—more than just typed sentences—your active participation is required. To clarify, it isn't about doing more, but stilling, allowing, and yielding to the guidance that is within you—making space to hear what you already have within and around you that wants to speak.

When we write from within our emerging guidance it allows you to access your own guidance and also receive. This is the essence of energetic awakening. You may feel more stilling by reading or more rising of guidance. You may get insights you've never had or openings for next steps in your life. You may have a phrase that begins to live inside of you and inform your choices or an opening to receive that allows you to support others along this journey.

This book is written for and by you if you choose to position yourself within your Sacred Centers and open your awareness to what is around you ready to offer guidance about who and what you truly are.

Positioning Dimensionally

As we journey together through the energetic awakening process you will eventually land in a position that is more than your centered space within—it is a more expansive, vibrational space. This landscape is larger than you and it opens into an expanse that is not only wise, but infinite. For now, imagine this space as something that surrounds you at all times. It is not flat nor has it only one way of being within it. It is a space where when we open into it, it is as though we are able to see various facets or reflections. You can take different orientations within the space that allows you to access energetic processes to move within and through you.

Science now points us toward a quantum universe where everything is energy. In energetic awakening you will place yourself within this larger space and you will learn how to navigate within it. Participation from within dimensional space is what opens you into it. Like walking through the woods on a narrow path that opens into an expansive vista, we enter dimensional space through energetic pathways that move us by being within them. In other words, larger space opens by centering within and then centering in the larger space beyond us. This is the pathway of opening.

We expand awareness as it opens us into this dimensional space. People seek this space through phenomenal occurrences of knowing where they have access to the unseen in spirit guides, angels, and energy. All of this is wonderful and we will give pointers for how to begin to access your own connection to the unseen realms. However, these connections are not what you might think. Mystical manifestations are simply reflections of something larger that is beckoning us all to come home. Access to them increases as we learn to position dimensionally.

We offer distinct movements that will support you along the journey so that you don't fall into the trap of efforting to make something open before it's time. To walk the energetic awakening path requires release. We cannot bypass the grief that must be met or the challenge and drudgery in the ordinary. To position dimensionally does not require ascension out of. Rather, it is a deepening into what is most routine—from within this larger space—that opens the energetic domain we seek. Our spiritual embodiment is the prime mover for allowing this space to open and it becomes the awakened landscape that we live in from this point forward.

Essence and Vibrational Energies

We are going to use some terms that sound a bit far out. Essence and vibration are two of them. As we listen in to the unfolding process of energetic awakening these are words that we wouldn't necessarily choose to use, but they so accurately represent the phenomena we are describing that we stick with them.

Our universe is light and vibration. You are light and vibration. Light and vibration make up the stuff of which we are made. Learning to track light and vibration will help you to feel your fullness from within your experience making your spiritual light (or essence) embodied (vibration) in the world. We need both of these qualities to manifest our highest self in this world.

Essence has a pure, clear quality to it. It often feels as though it comes from beyond and can move into our awareness at a moment's notice. You may remember a time when you felt that someone really understood you or that they were almost seeing through you in a way that made you somewhat uncomfortable. The directness was distinctly noticeable. Even with the discomfort, you may have found yourself feeling a fullness within you in the interaction. This direct, pure, cut to the heart of things captures essence.

We all have a soul essence that is often forgotten in the construction of the *You*, your ego— the pure, clear, reflection of what you are. In order to remember this essence quality, something has to spark within for essence to return and rise within us. You may get a sense of this feeling when holding a newborn baby or watching a beautiful sunrise or petting and deeply connecting with a beloved pet. These moments of experiencing the purity of essence are sparking for they remind us of the light of truth, who we truly are. When we work with the energetic movement of awakening, we actively allow essence to connect with each and every being we meet. Our light calls forward the light in another.

Embodiment in our lived experience carries a vibration. Think of it like cracks in the earth or streams of water that are making inroads through the ground. The purpose of vibration is to create receptivity and space within for awakening to land permanently. In this way, we cannot go back to sleep. Like gently using your finger to make space for a seed to be planted in the earth, vibration creates a readied space for essence to be planted. Vibration opens passageways for completion and readies energy for manifestation.

When we become aware of our vibration (both within and dimensionally), it allows the essence energy of awakening to land, allowing it to open within us and touch those around us. Too often, essence energy comes into your life, but it doesn't seem to do anything. An Ah-ha moment where something breaks in, a sense of fullness and wonder that alters how you see life and your circumstances simply disappears over time. Without vibration creating an opening, essence is often only a beautiful experience in a moment in time that slowly fades into a distant memory. The action of vibration takes essence and allows it to move into your lived experience. Like two connecting points, when essence meets vibration, permanent awakening occurs. We are reminded of what we truly are (essence) and it lands in our lived experience and it is hard to go back to sleep.

Through this process, you will tune to different qualities of light essence and vibrational spaces. We will give you pointers for tracking and opening space from within essence and vibration, but you have to feel it to get it. If you notice the mind questioning or shutting down simply follow the movement you will learn of stilling, allowing, and yielding in order to relax into rather than figuring out. You will be guided in the process and that is part of what is so special.

This book will help you position in a particular way within a higher vibration that will bring the unseen spaces much closer around you and allow essence to come through. You are fully supported in this process by the larger dimensional space that surrounds you. By practicing you are opening to that wise space where you will be met, tangibly and experientially.

Following the Path of Energetic Awakening

This process, while natural and simple, does require practice, which is specifically how energetic awakening is different. We gently point out the markers of awakening along your way, but the process you are tracking is within and around you. Each movement along the awakening path offers an opportunity to energetically orient to a new space and to deepen within it. The movement you will follow is one of release— stilling, allowing and yielding— and you will practice this over and over.

You will also become comfortable with the unseen. We will use energy as our guide to open this space and walk you into it, step by step. We have walked with many, many people who have followed the energetic awakening pathway and this process consistently opens people into what their heart most wants—to feel, see, and know what lies just beyond their sight. Part of seeing and knowing that which is unseen is also encountering that which we do not wish to see within ourselves. We do not bypass what is unwanted in this process. Rather, we learn to orient within our experiencing and to follow the unfolding movements.

And, if what you are most interested in is the opening of the mystical, subtle, and energetic realms, you will get that by engaging this process. What might surprise you is that there is more waiting for you beyond these experiences. Still, you will be able to access spirit guides, follow energetic movement, and connect with nature in sacred ways. The living landscape of the unseen will become a place of habitation and this process will support you in getting there.

This emerging awareness of energy is the practice for you to learn to be within the experience, following energetic movement from within. It takes time to distinguish the difference between being fully within an emerging energetic movement rather than standing slightly outside looking in. In the former the energy can move through you and teach you. In the later, the mind is in control and consequently the energy limits and flattens.

It takes repeated opportunities of dropping within your experiencing and staying with emerging energies—allowing essence to make contact through vibration—for energy to move and open. It's like training to ride a bike or learning a new skill. Practice allows for your overt knowing to become intuitive experiencing the more you abide in this space. It may take 100 times a day of noticing your mind coming back online and being just slightly outside of experiencing trying to observe and then dropping back in. Use the skills to provide hand holds along the way so that one day you don't even notice that you are almost always in center, tracking the energies within and around you.

So, don't skip the practices. We understand the tendency to read a book that has exercises and to simply skip them. We realize that many exercises feel like an add on for engagement and aren't very compelling. They certainly aren't worth stopping for any length of time.

The practices offered at the end of each section are the steps that must be walked for energetic awakening to be lived. They are the unfolding movements that allow energetic processes to open and guide you. If you skip them, you will miss the key to your opening. We've done our best to articulate the process in language that is understandable. We've held a particular vibration that is essential for the opening. But you have to do the practicing and it just takes time to orient. If you really don't want to do them from the book, we encourage you to access our free resources on our website and to do those meditations in their place. You need to be within the opening vibration that holds you throughout this process to learn to track energies from within.

Energetic Experiencing

You are a fullness of being, alive with communication and movement that can be known and accessed. It takes practice, but not the kind that evokes fatigue and striving. Let this first step be simple, more like play than work as you feel into these three simple, natural energetic movements.

1. Make Space: Take a moment and allow your *You* (your mind) to take a step to the side. You might not even know what that means yet, but simply visualize your mind resting quietly to the side of your experience, like putting your thoughts on a shelf. Your mind will be there for you to come back to later.

Another practice to make space is to draw a large circle around yourself in your imagination and put everything that is not you outside of that circle. You may begin to notice that there is simply more space without the crowding of your mind and life circumstances. In this space, feel yourself. Allow your experiencing to tangibly infuse the open space around you. This is your fullness. You are more than what you perceive.

2. Center: Begin to drop your awareness within. If your mind pops in and protests or says it doesn't know how to do that simply release, relax, and let your mind gently migrate back to its place outside of you as you hold these movements with love.

It is doing what minds do.

Place one hand in the middle of your chest, right in the center of your heart. Drop your awareness in that place. Feel it as a movement that is carrying you. Take a few moments to rest here. Then, place your other hand right over your navel. Drop your awareness softly to this second place within while also staying in your heart center.

You are within your Sacred Heart and Wisdom Centers simultaneously.

You may feel nothing, an essential aspect for awakening. It is in the nothing that we begin to know the something of the soul. This is a movement that is not built on doing it right. Rather, it will help you to orient to the energy of awakening within you. At this point you may begin to notice a sense of balancing within or that the mind is less chirpy. Hold this positioning. It is the positioning that encourages essence and vibration to meet.

3. Expand: From this position, begin to expand your awareness all around you—above, behind, below, ahead. It may feel like energy moving outward from you filling the space around you. This is a 360-degree movement. As you expand into the space around you, you do not leave your sacred centers. It is from these centers that we access the passageway to that which is unseen.

As you expand awareness, you may encounter the expectation within that you will feel something. That is of the mind. Simply release and allow your experience to guide you. Be within the movement of expansion and let it be the guide. Moments of fear may emerge as we live in ego constructs that limit our perception. As you expand awareness, let your experience be as it is and stay within the experience.

. . .

These movements are basic. Make space, center within, expand awareness. We cannot bypass these sequential movements. As we make space, the *You* quiets. When we center within we locate fully within the soul. When we expand our awareness, we allow the energetic movement of light and vibration. This is a sacred positioning that invites the *You* to lovingly quiet and the soul to speak. This is energetic awakening.

2

SPARKING AND CRACKING

Enter with us the world of Julian of Norwich. It is the 14th century in Norwich, England, a city filled with poverty, plague, and famine. An anchoress named Julian lives in a small cell and is known as a counsellor— one who offers advice to those who are in pain. She knows pain herself. On May 8th, 1373, Julian, aged 30, was lying on her presumed deathbed when she received the first of 16 visions. The vision is of Christ standing before her bleeding and emanating both complete suffering and complete love. From this she writes her work Revelations of Divine Love.

What Julian experienced was a crack that opened into a crevasse delivered through her suffering. This crack became a message that she communicated to others. Her message is a new revelation for all people — for all those who suffer—as she coined the memorable phrase, "All shall be well and all shall be well. All manner of things shall be well." Opening into this new awareness further, one of Julian's most famous revelations is a reference to Jesus as Mother where she points toward the nature of motherhood in understanding God's love for us. Julian meets through a sparking in her visions the energetic path into full awareness of the compassionate, eternal love of God and the steadfast knowing that "all shall be well." It is from this place that she then lives.

. . .

Energetic Awakening is about returning home to the truth of what you are. Our walk on this planet is similar in that each one of us is journeying back to a position within that allows us to live from the soul. Our paths can be varied and the steps to get there quite different and yet, there is a call that beckons each one of us to move out of the story we are living— the things we tell ourselves, the circumstances that have happened to us, the limiting beliefs that guide us—and to come home. Your life is constantly sparking you to come home—some invitations welcome and some at first unwelcome. All are sparks to come home.

Unearthing Soul Seeds

Awakening is about bringing to life an essential aspect of what you are. Each one of us has a universal soul seed that lies dormant within us, awaiting something that will allow it to grow. It does not matter where you come from or what form of spirituality you do or do not practice. The seed of your soul came with you in this incarnation and you will carry it with you when you go.

You may want to visualize this soul seed in your mind. Can you imagine a seed that is planted in autumn that rests quietly underground all winter? It isn't discontent in the waiting and it is not striving to germinate. It simply waits where it is for something to happen. When the conditions are right—temperature, rain, sunshine—something wakes up inside the seed and says, "Grow!"

So, too, with energetic awakening. There isn't any critique about when or how long it takes a seed to open. There isn't a spiritual timeline that must be achieved. The soul seed within each one of us can begin to germinate and then stop, begin again and then grow. It may grow and die back many times—like a perennial plant that goes dormant for winter to then rise again in the spring. The soul seed is ready at all times for growth, it simply needs the right conditions and an igniting impetus to begin to grow.

Enter into a parable about a seed and a sower. The context is that Jesus is teaching from a boat with a large crowd gathered by the shore. His first word at the beginning of the parable is, "Listen!" and his closing clap of words, "Let anyone with ears to hear, listen!" Feel even now the movement of these words, the reverberation of "listen" throughout your being. This is sparking, an energetic movement that is making its way to call forward the soul seed within. It is an opening that makes space for a greater awareness to rise within you.

The parables of Jesus are incredibly relevant teachings even for today. They break apart formed ways of thinking and offer repeated sparking to alight and break down. Parables serve to spark and open us into the ineffable— that which is beyond the mind. No matter how much you think about them, their meaning is not easily pinned down or captured. The messaging turns over something within us to make way for spirit. They were, and still are, confusing when met head on, but if you listen for the embedded teaching of awakening you begin to see. They speak directly to the soul and call it into the light of day.

Jesus paints the picture of seeds that fall upon the earth, some struggling to take root and grow in shallow, cracked soil. Others, burrowing deeper and deeper, soaking in nutrients, sun and water, and flourishing into living plants. So, it is with soul seeds that lie dormant within you. It is awareness of how the sparks—the call to pay attention— to take notice of what life is bringing your way, that open the rich good earth of soul abundance.

Hold awareness of Jesus's words. The spark of opening in the call to listen breaks through the chattering voice in your head—the part of you that is busy making lists and piling up worries. Feel how the crack, the opening of "Listen!" serves to make you pause, to wait and watch. From this opening, notice how the words settle deeper within and outside the understanding of your mind. You may not even understand what that story was about. Feel instead how something settles and opens within you. This is the essence of energetic movement beyond the mind. Then, feel how you are the soil. Feel your life as the ground to plant in. How receptive are you in your life? Can the energetic sparking movements get through? You may begin to feel the soil of your life and begin to relate with it in new ways, maybe as parched, cracked, sparse, or loamy. You are feeling within the movement of energy and it is showing you something experientially. It is breaking apart something formed so that energy can come through. You've just made space for the depth of the rich, good earth to invite you to live more fully into something more, an awaiting abundance and fullness.

Sleeping

Even though our soul awaits us, we can live a whole life without realizing this truth. It's like that feeling when driving. You've gone for miles and miles along the highway to all of a sudden realize you passed your exit ages ago. Where were you that you hadn't noticed? What was consuming you that your task of exiting wasn't forefront in your mind? Each one of us has patterns for how we go away into another space within where life runs on autopilot. We do what the world tells us we are meant to do and one day wake up and say, "Is this all there is? Isn't there more to this life?"

In order to have these reflective thoughts about your life, something must happen to remind you that you were looking for an exit in the first place and then to realize that you have already passed it. Without something jostling you out of your living trance you simply continue on as you always have. You end up in places you were never meant to go. You live with a sense of dis-ease and disappointment at the life you have unintentionally created.

Some traditions call this trance state living from within illusion. They describe it as a form of unconsciousness where we are asleep to life and need to wake up. This trance is simply a story that we tell ourselves that plays over and over and becomes a narrative about our lives and the larger world. We can live on autopilot for a very long time without noticing the story. We are sleeping and we don't even know it.

We know we are asleep when we live our life through a set of pictures, like flipping through photos on our phone, there is a projected awareness of what we are. There is the accountant. There is the college friend, the childhood friend, the party friend, the work friend. There is the sister, the daughter, the mom. These pictures become framed and we live in an objective relationship to them. We view them from the outside rather than living within them.

We can also spend a whole lifetime addressing the stories that have happened to us, trying to make them change by meeting them head on. As therapists we have each committed a significant portion of our personal and professional lives to working in this space. The goal in this form of work is for the stories to shift and for something to be radically altered. Too often, however, we simply end up continuing to live the pattern of the story dressed up in new clothing. We tell it over and over and instead of transforming, it gets stuck on repeat. The hum of our sleepiness or the repetition of the story keeps us deadened to what lies below.

Living Mentally

And this is one of the keys. You cannot simply awaken through the mind. To awaken into a different kind of living you must alter where you engage the world so that you don't miss the off-ramp awaiting you in life. We cannot think our way out of our sleepy state. We must learn to track a process that places us differently within our life.

You may already know that the mind is not all that you are. There may be many moments of serendipity in your experience where something more was happening— a business deal came through at just the right time and place, a check arrived for you to make that payment, or someone you were thinking about called out of the blue. You may tell yourself that it was coincidence or the cleverly crafted words in your proposal, but another part of you knows it was something more than that. There is a larger energetic movement that you are part of that goes far beyond your intellect. You may not know exactly how to describe it, but some part of you knows it energetically and intuitively.

Billionaire Warren Buffett calls this awareness his inner scorecard. While our world is programmed to assess from the outside using spreadsheets and data or to consider what others might think about this or that, Buffett says the most essential location in which we make decisions is from within.

You may be thinking, as the mind does, that without your rational mind to assess you wouldn't have much to live from. The mind has a rightful place as the one who acts— your thinking gets done what another part of you requests. Our minds are an important part of what makes us human. We certainly wouldn't want to get rid of them. The challenge is to put the mind in its rightful place where it is in service to the soul, not the other way around.

This is not easy. Not only does the world elevate the place of the thinking mind. Too often spirituality does as well. We are trained to think our way out of pain. The mind is tricky. Just when you think you've mastered something mentally, life throws you a curveball. And that's the issue. Our spiritual lives must gain traction in our everyday life to affect the kind of change that energetic awakening requires.

And yet, here is the sticking point, you will never wake up to the soulful person that you are through your mind alone. To simply awaken mentally isn't enough. You may think a lot about exits and off-ramps, but you won't get off the road at the right time if that is all you are accessing.

Energetic awakening supports you in learning to live from a new place within, where you have access to another form of knowing that changes how you engage the world. This process will move you out of your storied illusions and give you the power to change the patterns and behaviour that you yearn to shift. This embodied process teaches you to track inner movements and the larger unseen spaces around you in a way where you stay awake. To be within the unfolding experiencing of any moment is what the journey is about.

Sparking

We don't know the exact moment that a seed wakes up. We can only watch the movements that happen once it awakens by a spark in life. We may not be able to track our own awakening with clarity, but we can learn to watch the markers that point toward the growth that is about to break forth.

As we noted, there is always a spark that lights the soul seed within. Sparks are simple moments of in-breaking where the ordinary movements of life are altered in some way that awakens the soul seed within. The moment could be now, right here, as you read these words for it doesn't take much, just a spark, just some open space in your life experience. All that is needed is for you to pause long enough to let the light break through just a little and illuminate something dormant resting deep within you. This is when a crack opens.

The sparking is a catalyst that gets things going. A spark can be anything, literally. A spark can be a circumstance that gets you to notice your life in a different way. It can be a suffering that you experience that deepens you into an emotion within. A spark can be a one-time occurrence or a repeated knocking at your door. The possibilities are endless —from the warming of the sun on your life's ground to an earthquake that wakes you up out of your slumber and gets your attention—sparks come in all kinds of packages.

For us, we now recognize many sparks dotting our life path that once went unnoticed. Many were simple openings that allowed us to stop long enough to observe the spaces in-between where a deeper part within us was beckoning. And yet, we also have others that were dramatic, many of which were considered unwelcome. Each one helped to spark our soul seed and invited us to grow toward awakening.

A spark is not something you can control or make happen. It may show up during a period of glorious wonder, and it is just as likely to arrive during a time of deep grief or boring activity. We can utter words out loud to one another, such as hawk, landscape, moving, job, or falling, and though they are tied to a story that unfolded in our lives, it is more the symbolic resonance they carried and the purpose that they served in our awakening that is essential. Each of these words refer to a spark in our life that watered the soul seed and invited us to grow.

Sparks can occur intentionally as well. Bold leadership can evoke cracks that spark awakening systemically. Symbol and metaphor can serve to crack open old patterning into new life. In 1995 Nelson Mandela stood into the emerging unity of South Africa by attending the Rugby World Cup wearing a Springboks' jersey, both representing apartheid. Standing in front of the crowd, he gave the clenched fist salute of the ANC (African National Congress), appealing to the Black South African movement. The two symbols that he wore and enacted, opened a moment in history.

The mind will take these sorts of sparks that emerge and will paste many faces of logic onto them to cover over the rupture. Being within what is nonsensical will widen the gap for the soul to emerge. It makes no logical sense for the leader of Black South Africa to wear a white supremacy jersey. It is this nonsensical action that serves to open the soul. Do not discount how your commitment to not patch over the cracks in your life serve as cracks for others.

As you learn to tune yourself to their message, you will begin to see sparks everywhere, dotting your path along the way. In looking back now, it isn't how large or small or even the content of the sparks that mattered. It was the space created within us for something wiser to emerge. The key is learning to listen and notice the sparks for what they are and to learn to live life from a position where we follow these sparks as guidance in all of life.

Sparking in the Everyday

Often when we talk about spirituality, we expect the extraordinary. We look to places in our lives where big things happen, such as where we find God, experience the Divine, or are captured by wonder. We train ourselves to look for the glorious rather than the ordinary and as a consequence we may miss what is already before us in our experience.

Sparking can arrive just as easily while doing laundry or eating a meal with a friend as it can in a moment of transcendence. We have to retrain our eye to notice the small things in life and to begin to explore the spaces between our experience. It is the interstitial spaces—the space in-between what we see with our eyes—that sparks and opens awakening. Noticing is the first step to allow the spark to move you.

Nature was often a catalyst in our own energetic awakening. She taught us to slow down and quiet just long enough to begin to hear. We weren't thinking about making anything happen. Rather, we were compelled to wake up, walk outside, and listen. Every day we walked in quiet without expectation. The more we walked in silent space, the more the space opened. No expectation. No Intention. We simply walked.

Rising whisperings from within the aliveness of our surroundings began to speak and over time we heard and saw more and more that sparked within us. We seemed to need the liminal space of emerging dawn to quietly awaken us from within. We learned to track our experiencing from within the connected space of nature. She naturally held and opened us with each footfall and bird song.

They can even be simpler than that. You may notice yourself folding laundry more mindfully or being within the dish drying and number crunching in a different way. What once was on autopilot now has a level of reflection with it. This is making space. Various aspects of the everyday simply feel different. And here's the key, you begin to notice. The space that noticing creates is enough for a spark to make its way through anything.

Extraordinary Sparking

A spark can also show up with a bang. Large life events tend to get our attention in a way where the ordinary might not. These events can be tragic and they can also be wondrous. It is the visibility and force of these sparks that stick. When life gets our attention through the dramatic it anchors our experiencing in a tangible way.

We have worked with many people who know these life

sparks and can directly name them. These are the moments where they wake up to something about life. They might be reflections, such as "How I feel now is amazing and I want more of this." Or, "This pain of loss is so searing I can't stand it. I have to do something." Or, "How did this happen? I lost everything I've been working for. Now what do I do?" Events that impact us stick around in our bodies and they can be the spark that launches us forward into a willingness to look at life in a different way.

Some part of you may resonate with these words and know already the moments that have sparked you to notice life differently or helped you to pause long enough to see from a new perspective the familiar terrain you have walked over and over. Noticing the upsets and events make you pay attention. These unexpected events can be large or small. It may have been a loss or change in job or location. It may have been something upsetting happening in your relationship, or something done to you. Or it simply could be waiting yet again on the freeway in traffic aware of time ticking away that caught your attention. It could be a dismal second quarter or an unexpected boom that comes out of nowhere. Again, the circumstances don't matter. It is the space these in-breaking moments provide through the noticing.

Whether your story is filled with dramatic events, everyday moments, or a combination of both, they are there for you to uncover, allowing you to position yourself differently in relation to your life. You may not know it, but the spark is moving you and the unwelcome can become the catalyst for the change you long for most. Do not limit what the spark is. Simply notice what is arriving.

Cracking

Sparks enliven the soul seed to begin to expand and grow. These sparks open cracks of awareness in our life, a movement out of illusion. Cracks can be facilitated by making space within for the spark to move more freely. Practices of space making include meditation, reflection, exercising, or rest. However, often a spark breaks through the unwanted cracks of awareness in your life to open you to a different way of perceiving and knowing that begins to move you.

In 2004, ABC News Anchor Dan Harris was reporting the news updates at the top of the hour. In front of five million people, he began to experience symptoms of a panic attack. Watching the footage, the panic in his eyes was apparent before he quickly stated, "back to you" and bailed on the newscast. From this experience, which he called a "crack," he acknowledged that he had been "sleepwalking through a cascade of moronic behavior." He became a reluctant convert to meditation for a basic reason. It was good for his brain and tamed the voice in his head. Even a crack can open what is soulfully rational within us. No matter what or how, it is still a crack that is emerging because of a sparking within you.

Cracks emerge over time through the persistence of sparks in our life until we cannot turn away. They break apart something solid, and like a dam that holds back tremendous water pressure, a single crack can be enough to release a great force. What makes a life crack is often the unexpected, the messes and mistakes of daily living. We call them cracks because they break apart what once felt solid and allow a light to shine through. This breaking apart can happen in times of wonder and awe. You may find that you name them as spiritual and welcome them as inspiration. Too often, however, it is the challenges and unwanted deliverances of life that create the cracks. You may describe these as painful and unwelcome for they challenge your well-ordered life.

We all know a story of someone, maybe even you, who met something in their life that forever changed them. These are the rags to riches or overcoming hardship stories we love. Maybe they became a parent for the first time and the workaholic tendencies redirected them back to their home life. Maybe someone experienced a significant loss in their family and they gave up their corporate career path and started a bakery. What occurred is less important than the movement that emerged from the event. An energetic movement sparked something within them and they acted. Their life cracked open from there.

Cracking in the Everyday

Too often we remember only the big moments of life that opened a crack in our awareness and we overlook the awakening cracks present in the everyday. The odd conversation on a bus that is calling you home. Mowing the grass on a Saturday and finding a rare stillness within that is calling you to return. Every movement of every day is an energetic beckoning for you to pay attention to the soul seed that is within you. It requires your awareness, moreover, an awareness that allows you to see what the mind would call nothing. There isn't anything that happens in your life that is irrelevant. Everything is something. Too often, we feel these simple moments of opening and we rationalize them away. We felt that stillness when we were mowing because we were in a rhythm. That's it. Or, the guy on the bus was just a one-time conversation. It wasn't anything.

We begin by allowing our inner awareness to notice, whether through a panic attack or a simple moment of silence. We make just enough space for the energetic movement of sparking to come through and break into a crack so that we recognize these moments everywhere. No longer do we dismiss and overlook. We have now paused long enough for something more to come through.

In our experience, these cracks are persistent. Many times we reduced them to mere circumstance, such as an illness, a financial stress, the loss of a job, the strain of a relationship. Instead of glossing over them with the paint of reasoning, view them as invitations to awaken, to open space that unveils a new reality. We see cracks for what they truly are, not how we named them. It is the piling up of these sparks that open the larger crack that finally captures our attention.

Jesus is the embodiment of repeated and persistent cracks. He foretells Peter's denial of him with blistering directness. "You will disown me," Jesus says. Peter insists that he will not and repeatedly smooths over the probability of his actions. The servant girl says to Peter, "You were with him!" The words of denial flow swiftly and easily from Peter's mouth. The crack is unrelenting. Again, the servant girl calls him out saying, "You are one of them." With greater insistence, Peter paints it over once again. "I am not." Finally the pressure increases. A crowd emphatically calls him, even naming his accent as the dead giveaway. The rise in Peter is equally forced, "I do not know the man!"

The crack opens fully and Peter weeps. Even in this breaking open, there is still the mind's persistence to clean up and repair. Again, an hour later another asks about his association to Jesus and Peter denies it again with bitter tears of anguish. Yet, Peter is beloved, a cherished disciple as errant as he is portrayed. The cracks open a deeper state of love and devotion within Peter, to the point where he is later charged by Jesus to feed his sheep, tend to his ministry, and live his legacy as a commissioned disciple.

Discount nothing in this process for anything can be used to create just enough space. You do not make this process move, for it is a moment of grace that breaks in. These kinds of sparks happen over and over continually throughout your life as you live within energetic awakening. It is the moment of grace where what is most true about who and what you are meets that which surrounds and supports you at all times. From that meeting the seed within begins to grow.

The perspective we now have allows us to see these inbreakings, events that happened in our lives, as the spaces that moved and opened us to awakening. Even what we called unwanted—disturbances and unfortunate occurrences— shift when seen from this larger perspective.

Letting Light Out

Remember, the reason for the cracks is to let something open. It is your soul. Too often life is like a walking trance that is living you forward as you go through the motions of each day. Whether you are on autopilot or actively creating life in the image you imagine it should be, life moves you in an automatic way that covers over the openings of spirit. Whatever you call it, life needs a way to get your attention. It is often the smallest of cracks that begins the process of awakening.

It's only when life breaks in that the trance is permanently broken. All of those unexpected events, the things that didn't quite fit, the feeling in your gut of something not quite right, foretold the arrival of something that awakens you and breaks you out of your trance to get your attention. The carefully hung pictures on the wall of your life begin to tilt and fall. All of a sudden you can no longer do things the way you always have and what you once found comforting and familiar no longer is. Words that used to flow from your tongue get trapped within and you can't abide in spaces that are familiar anymore. You may try to smooth things over or scold yourself for bad behavior, but when you really pay attention, you recognize that it is no longer about you, but about what is waking up within you.

Calling You Home

The call to return is the same for everyone for the message is universal. You are being prompted to break out of the illusions you hold about what life is and to begin seeing life from a different perspective. The universal call home is the most consistent, persistent, repeated invitation throughout all of time.

Know that as you draw breath each day with an awareness that is pointing toward a deeper reality, you are being returned home. As you are willing to stop and listen, you will notice it emerging on your path for it is already there. Even if all you sense is a taste or a whisper, know that something is evolving even if all you can do is scratch the surface. You won't be able to name the moment of return saying, 'Ahh, this is the moment when I was being asked to come home' because it is already there.

Energetic Experiencing

Every moment in life holds the capacity for a seed to break ground within you. Do not effort to find them. They are already there waiting for your awareness to rest lightly on the spark of light that is ready to break forth. There may be fear as it is unknown how these sparks may alight in your life. Light will break forth when we are present and patient with the spark that wishes to become a flame. Even if it feels like a hint or glimmer or barely a flicker, know that to live is to carry these sparks.

1. **Center:** Follow the energetic awakening movements. Make space, center within, expand awareness. Rest in this positioning. Allow an awareness of a time in your life that sparked your soul to come forward. Do not strive to find the perfect moment or one you think is a sparking experience. Trust that what your soul speaks to you is the right moment for you. Open to what is rising.
2. **Withinness:** Be within the experience that is emerging. There may be moments when the mind rises and you find yourself standing outside of the experience, like an observer. Go back within. Feel the movement of the experience without assessment or judgment. There may be emotion that begins to rise. Follow this energetic movement and welcome it as a friend. It is guiding you into the spark.
3. **Stay:** Stay present in your experiencing and let it begin to move you. You may see how this moment in time is actually more than a memory. It is alive and vibrant and present in the moment you are in. You are following the energy rather than the form of this experience. Let the energetic movement of a spark that fans into a flame of awakening guide you. You may find that the movement changes, as you are not remembering but actively engaging in this spark. It is getting rewritten or re-shaped. Allow the energy to show you the truth of what is sparking and opening within. You will know if your mind is guiding you if the experiencing starts to close or contract. It will continue to open when you step into the energetic flow. Notice and allow. There will be a sense of stilling or quieting of the

energetic movement when the soul has sparked and opened.

The sparks of the soul are infinite for to live is to return home. All of life is a spark. You need not remember a mountaintop experience in order to notice how the cracks are opening. Hold awareness even after the meditation. Who or what is present in your life now that is a reflection or an invitation to live deeper? We promise you that they are there. Open to this idea that even what you may define as unwelcome in your experience is a call to come home. From this positioning, it is possible to see what has been hidden in plain sight. You are beloved and whole and there is a presence awaiting you in everything.

3

MISMATCHING AND MISSTEPS

You likely know something about Mary Magdalene, no matter what tradition you come from. Her legacy has endured and her story has been told throughout the ages. Mary Magdalene is mentioned twelve times in the Gospels, more than any other woman and she was with Jesus at his death. She has been depicted as everything from a prostitute to a celibate nun. She is followed as a feminist icon and in recent years has been rendered as the partner or passive helpmate of Jesus. Whatever story we believe, it is most likely not true in its current telling because the facts of her life are not well known. What we do know is that she was a valued woman—an apostle— at a time in history when women were looked down upon. Gospel and apocryphal writings say she understood the teachings of Jesus when others did not understand. This is her mystique. Her presence among the disciples was a mismatch, something that at first did not fit, and yet her message rings forward today.

We do not even know if this is the Mary referred to in this scene, but imagine the context and feel the drama that unfolds. Mary is with Jesus, gathered around them are other disciples and family members. She unexpectedly takes an alabaster jar of precious ointment and falls to the ground. Mary pours the precious oil on the feet of Jesus and begins kissing them. Can you feel how this act of love and gratitude led Mary to act despite her surroundings? With others looking on, likely horrified at the cost of the ointment being wasted and the visible, public display of emotion, Mary continues. She is within something so powerful that she can do nothing but continue and to show what is present and filling her heart.

You are beginning to notice life differently and this may surprise you. Instead of life simply humming along as it always has—eating meals, going to work, enjoying weekends—you begin to attend to the spaces in between action. The senses that rise are capturing your attention in a new way. Something out of sync catches your eye. An expected event that doesn't go the way it always has. The smooth rhythm of your work day gets interrupted with spills and tears and flat tires. Life begins to hiccup instead of flow smoothly in the ordinary things of life.

We expect spiritual movement to be paired with enjoyable emotions like a glorious sense of wonder and transcendence. More often than not at this point in the journey, it is a sense of out-of syncness, an emerging disorder that is most evident. Even if you've had a powerful, awe-inspiring awakening spark, your return to the everyday will be enough to catapult you back into something less smooth that requires an ongoing attentiveness.

You may have a sense of this in your own life. Have you ever gone on a retreat or vacation, experienced something profoundly moving or beautiful, and felt the reluctance to return home or leave the situation? It's as if the context you are in is holding something precious that you know you will lose if you exit the space.

It is similar to this point on the journey. You catch the first glimmers of life lived differently—the cracks opened enough space for something else to get your attention, allowing more of life to come through. What follows right on its heels is a sense of mismatch in the everyday. It may simply be snags in the smooth, silk fabric of life, but these moments are experienced as disruptive and unwanted.

Making Messes

Life gets messy when you awaken. Everything that is not of the soul begins to break apart and you start seeing your daily experience in a new way. The cracks become larger. The dis-ease stronger. The sense of disorientation grows. Because your perspective is shifting, you go to what you know for explanation—your circumstances—even though they don't help to make sense of what is happening anymore.

The disorientation of awakening can feel like getting lost in the woods. Legend tells of a little boy named Paul who in 1805 went hunting for sarsaparilla on the shores of Lake Ontario. While out hunting for this herb, he became disoriented in the thick woods and he couldn't find his way home. His family searched tirelessly for three days, but after no sign of Paul they believed he was dead.

Paul recalled his family saying they lived approximately 40 miles from Niagara, New York. This memory was Paul's guide. When he was able to find his way out of the thick forest he found the edge of a lake to follow as his navigation. Paul jammed a stick in the ground each night before falling asleep to stay oriented in the right direction in case he awoke confused. Days later, Paul stumbled into Niagara, NY to the great surprise and joy of his family.

Like being turned around in the woods, the awakening journey can feel scrambled and disorienting. We use small sticks to orient us, markers to guide us while we make our way from the world we have known into the new world that is emerging. We can cling to these sticks of normalcy as we navigate uncharted space and they can help us find our way through all of the mess.

The messiness is both necessary and intentional, and it isn't comfortable. It is likely the most disorienting place on the awakening path because you no longer have the handholds you once did. You do not yet have an inner sense of rightness to rely on within yourself.

We hear people say "My life feels like it is collapsing. I don't know what is going on. Get me off this ride!" And that is a good metaphor. It can feel like the sparking of your soul seed delivered you to a roller coaster ride you didn't buy a ticket for. Your soul said yes to the ride, of that you can be sure, but as the bar goes down and the car inches it's way up the steep track, you wonder if there is any way to get off. You might find yourself blaming or complaining. And, you will likely look to your circumstances as the solution or source of your pain.

Stalling Awakening

Awakening processes often stall here for two reasons. One, it is uncomfortable and it feels like something has gone terribly wrong. Without support and an orienting guide to help you, folks often put themselves back to sleep and return to life as it once was. They simply get off of the ride.

In June 2016, The Atlantic published an article by Stephen Cave titled *"There's No Such Thing as Free Will: But we're better off believing in it anyway."* The article asserts that the laws of nature are predictable and conscious action stems entirely from the brain. Outrage quickly ensued as counterpoints and arguments peppered the editorial board. To assert the lack of free will upends our long held Western belief that we are in control of our destiny. Part of the awakening journey is facing that while we are able to consciously choose our path, we are not in control of it.

While this article may pop our bubble of optimism that we make choices entirely from outside forces and influences, it does speak directly to the prerogative we feel to get off the ride of awakening. We are wired for stability, security, and self-preservation and we innately follow natural order. Staying awake is a choice, and one that the article emphasizes in abundance. We are creative, reasonable and deliberate human beings that have the capacity to generate options. Staying aboard or jumping ship on the awakening journey is the root of free will and the ability to consciously choose which direction to take.

This can happen once or it can happen over and over. The awakening process is sparked, but somehow this stage of experiencing is never walked through. Energetic awakening requires a full-life overhaul with no stone left unturned. Without support, the sleepiness of routine returns and we slumber as a way to avoid the pain and unknowns inherent in awakening.

The other impediment is the mind. Here is where the ego, what you will engage is your *You*, pops online and convincingly guides you back to safe waters. Keep it abstract, separate, and clean. Don't allow your life to show the messy effects of dismantling. The mind plays tricks on us and the voice is so familiar we assume it is the only one talking to us. Over time you will learn to listen to another rising voice, but for now, the mind is ready to convince you to return to safer shores.

We felt that in our own lives. Our minds told us that we had to get-it-together, to stop the process that was dismantling our lives. There were plenty of inner conversations about how we would look to the world and how dangerous this path might become. We, too, wanted our lives to move seamlessly and not to look like a wreck, but these messes were the very catalyst we needed to chart our course forward, toward awakening, and the mind had to be bypassed to allow what no longer worked to fall away.

Falling Away

There is a rightness to the falling away that the mind can't quite grasp. When you view it straight on it feels wrong. How could dismantling be good? Things falling apart— your house of cards blown down? But, this season isn't without a purpose, one that supports us in navigating through rocky terrain to the other side. Life faithfully delivers what is required to undo what needs to be undone. Energetic awakening supports our continuing on even when it is difficult.

Energetic awakening invites it all. Because we work within experiencing, allowing our centered home base to support us, we learn to ride the waves of release from within the experience, not from without, and that becomes the movement forward. The challenges of our life become the training ground for staying positioned within center no matter the outer circumstances. Positioning is everything and this season helps to solidify this repeated return.

We can tell you with sincerity that this season wasn't comfortable. If we were sitting over coffee, Annie would tell you about resisting inner nudges to make changes and the repercussions of unfortunate decisions and money down the drain. Annmarie might begin her story with three literal, easily avoidable falls that slammed her to the ground, injured her and forced her into her first energy session. We have many stories that today we can tell while smiling, but it didn't feel funny at the time. This season may be filled with grumbling and a lot of head shaking, for while you are in the midst of the mess, it often doesn't make any sense.

. . .

Imagine Simon Peter announcing that he is going fishing with some other disciples. They spend a long night casting their nets, but their nets are empty come morning. Weary from lack of sleep, muscles aching, and ready for sleep, they see an approaching figure coming towards them on the sandy shoreline. It is Jesus that awaits them, but they do not recognize who he is. When he asks them, "Did you catch anything?" they laugh incredulously. Can he not see their aching hands, bleary eyes, and empty nets? Jesus calls again to them to throw their nets to the right side of the boat and see what happens. They cast their nets over the right side and as they do they are almost pulled overboard. Their nets are filled to overflowing with fish. There are so many fish it is impossible to bring their haul to shore.

As we awaken we may feel as though we are casting our nets over and over in the same spot, logically assessing our situation and chiding ourselves that something is not working any longer. Yet, the draw to continue in the same place, same time, same way compels us on. We are being called to look in a different direction and go a new way. It is the empty nets over and over again that finally push us to see what has been there all the time. There is abundance, new life, a new way of seeing our world that is just on the other side.

For us, the mess got so tangled at times that the only thing we could do was laugh. How in the world was this happening to a life that was so perfect and well-ordered? We marveled at how quickly that which had been buttoned-up could come undone. From renovations that went off track and descended into financial and circumstantial chaos to coveted jobs that no longer fit, and long nights with little sleep where we felt slightly crazy from exhaustion. We lived within this landscape for long seasons, even years. In many ways, whatever we tried to straighten just bent back out of shape again. We learned, over time, to simply allow. The more we straightened up and ironed out, the greater the disorder.

This is exactly why the process can feel so messy. Your life is breaking apart and breaking in. We, too, named things messy at the time because we were attached and sometimes clinging to what was happening. All the while, assessing what it meant. Often it was the discomfort that stopped us long enough, and then nudged us to look at the opening within the delivered circumstance. Once we released our internal dialogue about why and what was happening, we were able to lean in and listen below the outward mess to the divine communication below.

Making Things Right?

Your first instinct as this process opens within you might be to smooth over or pacify the life disruptions that are creating ripples and tears in the fabric of your existence. The initial urge is to right what has gone wrong and you will likely have a whole list of reasons why that is a good idea.

Moreover, others around you may encourage you to get-it-together and set yourself right for you are impacting them as well. We can't place an expectation on others to understand and support us in this process. Unless they too have walked this path, it looks like a cliff's edge to move away from, not one to embrace. People may question you and conflicts can occur because of all of the wrongly fitting pieces that can't be put right.

Rather than pacifying these disruptions you are invited to take notice of their presence with an awareness that they are pointing you homewards. For, it isn't actually the circumstances that you experience that are messy in this process, it's your association to them as being painful that makes them messy. When you identify with your circumstances, the events that are occurring within and around you, it solidifies something, making it into a "thing" that you then engage. The process of identification emphasizes the *who* rather than the *what* within and this creates the pain that you experience.

Embracing What No Longer Fits

If you think about it, it makes sense. All of the upending and dis-ease is causing you to pay attention. Your life has become one large crack where tremendous amounts of potential are pouring through. It may not feel like it right now, but the upset is intentional. You are allowing something to break in that otherwise could not.

The impetus to go back to the way things were may increase. You may find you want to go back to sleep just to avoid the pain. You may also find a rising inclination to neaten and tidy life as the dishes pile up in the sink with no time to wash them and the unexpected bills arrive with no idea where they came from or how to pay them. You will notice that everything is out of sync and you may become very aware of the outside eyes that are watching you.

According to Daeyoel Lee, Yale's Dorys McConnell Duberg Professor of Neuroscience and Professor of Psychology and Psychiatry, if we are not encountering a new and unfamiliar circumstance or information, our "learning center" or frontal cortex activity is dramatically reduced. Leaning into uncertainty primes us to not just awaken, but also learn a new way of being, thinking, and behaving in our world.

In many ways, what no longer fits is your spiritual invitation to step more solidly on the cracks of life's sidewalk and live deeply from within the dis-ease. You may wonder whether you are tempting fate as your shoe gets caught on life's uneven road and you find yourself constantly stumbling forward. You may feel an impulse to right yourself, to dust yourself off and look around to make sure no one is looking, and to carry on as you always have.

Don't. Notice your stumbling steps. Take heed of what no longer fits. The fantasy of perfection is a desire to live within a still life painting that does not move. We try to organize and orchestrate a scene of perfection. We can sustain it for a while, maybe even a lifetime, but eventually the picture cracks and fades, for real life is lived in the emerging now—the alive conversation of creation that unfolds in each divinely inspired moment. Pay attention to the new spaces within and the rising sense of rightness that is leading you down this new path. The waymaker is the mess, for you have finally broken out of your illusion, ready to inhabit the real life that awaits you.

The classic children's story of Goldilocks and the three Bears very simply and concretely depicts this feeling of noticing what no longer fits. Like Goldilocks, we are trying out three different chairs, one too big, one too soft and one that is just right. Or, tasting porridge that is too hot, too cold and one that is just right. The sense of what is right for each of us is changing. What we have known as a seamless fit no longer falls into place, hand in glove. What we once knew as a perfect fit no longer does and we are testing out where and how we fit in our life and the world moving forward.

It is time to embrace what no longer fits about your life. What may surprise you is the speed with which the mismatch was delivered to you. Or, it might be just the opposite. Your life path may be dotted with one broken thing after another, all signs to pay attention to that you've never noticed before. Actually, if you look back over your life from this vantage point you are likely to see a narrative unfold that isn't about the circumstances you've lived, but one that shows opportunities for awakening dotted regularly throughout.

To carry on as you always have is no longer an option for something larger is asking you to notice and to embrace what is both familiar and unfamiliar in the same breath. It is a call to say that you have been this way before, and you will go this way again. It is the call to continually look beyond what is, for the signs and signals that are calling you to return back home to the truth of what you are.

Energetic Experiencing

There is a movement in these moments of disorientation no matter how uncomfortable they may be. You cannot step around the missteps to find sure footing anymore. Being within the falls and stumbles are where you will find the guidance that awaits you. Even these words may feel uncomfortable. For, who wishes to stumble? But, it is by embracing what is, accepting that which is unwelcome, and releasing expectation that your steps become the pathway you will follow.

Even now, can you suspend what you believe to be 'not working' in your life and accept that it is. What is not working is guidance speaking directly to you.

1. **Center:** Find your centered positioning and notice how this position is a little more natural and familiar. Even if it feels like you don't yet understand what it means to be in position, in your center, simply place your hands on your Heart and Wisdom Centers and simply allow. Accept that over time this position will become the place from which you live. Be still. In this position there is nothing for you to do. The

dissonance in your life is welcome here. Accept everything and resist nothing. You need not effort. The rest you have been longing for is here.

2. **Accept:** There is a restlessness within you to find sure footing again. Go within this itchiness and acknowledge it. Allow it to be present. Resistance may rise to encourage you to step out of the discomfort. To do something to make the process shift or change. Stay present. It is within acceptance of this moment where you will experience release. You may need to breathe deeply into the acceptance, following the energetic flow within your body, for it is not the nature of the mind to allow this form of release. It is the essence of the soul, however, to let everything be as it is.

3. **Release**: Stay within the experience for the dissonance you experience is your passageway. It has emerged from the cracks and it is here to guide you. Soften into it and follow its movement of release. You may experience it as intensifying before it settles. Continue to soften your edges as you locate the shifting movements within. Notice how the movement is carrying you and stay present to the energy that is clearing and opening. You are doing nothing. Presence moves everything. Wait for the movement of settling, stillness, and completion. Feel each of these from within. A settling—a resting sense within. An emerging quiet where there is no thing—space, darkness, rest. A sense of completion—you are now within completely.

4

VACILLATING VOICES

The mystical voice can emerge from complete solitude and isolation giving it a sharpness and clarity unadulterated by the surrounding world. St Antony of Egypt's voice did just this. He lived in the 3rd century and much of his existence was living in isolation. Even though he rarely left his desert dwelling, his message was received by the larger world and today he is referred to as Antony the Great…

St. Antony struggled mightily with what he called the Devil (or his inner voice of You) and he spent nights in prayer, he fasted every other day, and he ate only bread and water. Through these practices he sought to enhance his devotion to God and to find a renewed purity. He saw his struggle as the vacillation between good and evil and he engaged this battle within his solitary desert chamber.

St. Antony only left his desert solitude twice. Even though he remained alone, his influence grew and others began to flock to the desert chambers to grow the community of the Desert Mothers and Fathers. Most remarkably, St Antony's teachings on choosing goodness in the vacillation between purity and evil spread without him actively engaging with the wider world. He inspired others to find their own position of center in between the pull between right and wrong. His most famous teaching encourages finding stillness as the way forward to shift from ego to soul. He writes, "Wherever you find yourself, do not go forth from that place too quickly. Try to be patient and learn to stay in one place."

In this season of upending you will begin to hear a new voice rise within you. It may at first sound like the chatter that talks to you in repetitive loops in your mind. Listen a bit more closely. There is another voice that is rising and it sounds and speaks quite differently. This is the voice of your soul. It is rising from the newly opened space within you and your job is to tune-in to it.

You may name them as two voices to enable you to grasp their distinctness and continue to feel into what separates them. In this way, you glimpse an emerging awareness of the deeper state that is now opening within you as the voices become more distinct. What you have called *You*, your identity that has defined you up until this point, is separating from the voice of your soul and as a consequence there are now two distinct voices within you—one of the ego (*You*) and one of the **soul.**

Numerous traditions talk about the ego—the self that guides you in life. The spiritual path requires a quieting of that voice for another awareness to come forth. This process can be referred to as a consciousness shift or a moment of awakening where the ego falls away. We see it as an energetic, embodied process where the ego *You* isn't eradicated but gentled into quieting. As you listen more fully to the wisdom of the soul, the ego can relax and allow more information and guidance to rise from the soul space.

A great deal of healing work addresses the ego. We have personally spent many years living within the story of the *You* voice with advanced training that helped us skillfully walk with others to find healing and symptom relief by engaging the stories lived through the ego. While this form of work is important, it is distinct from energetic awakening.

You cannot quiet the ego by directly engaging with it. It just won't work.

It's not that the *You* is unwanted. Rather, by learning the difference between the *You* and the soul, you have new awareness and access to a deeper process within that will open the world in a new way. You are tuning your ear to the voice of the soul so that you hear it when it speaks. All of the cracks and messes have been and will continue to be opportunities to tune your ear to the difference. Instead of living within your responses to your circumstances, the space that noticing creates helps you to hear the difference.

Recognizing the Voice of Your YOU

The voice of your *You* is invested in maintaining the life you've created. It is the voice that has kept you moving and gets tasks done each day. There is often a tone associated with this voice that you will learn to listen for. It may be demanding and push you to achieve. It may be critical, requiring ongoing action and a change of course when life doesn't look right or familiar. It will often counsel maintaining balance and not rocking the boat. And, how you are perceived by others and the larger world is of paramount importance. Look stable, put together, successful, like everyone else. If you are going to stand out, do so for your accomplishments, not for creating a disaster and a visible mess.

There are other distinctives of your *You* that will come forward as you recognize what is of the ego and what is the soul. There will be a tone that this voice uses. Many describe it as harsh and demanding. For some it is syrupy sweet and enticing. The voice can change qualities, shifting back and forth, but the demand that control is maintained is always present.

Perhaps one of the most poignant ancient stories

depicting the two voices is the Cherokee teaching of the two Wolves. This story depicts the vacillating voices within and demonstrates our agency to lean into the voice we wish to nurture.

In the tale, an elder Cherokee is teaching his grandson about life. "A fight is going on inside me," he says to the boy. "It is a terrible fight and it is between two wolves. One is evil — he is anger, envy, sorrow, regret, greed, arrogance, self-pity, guilt, resentment, inferiority, lies, false pride, superiority, and ego. The other is good — he is joy, peace, love, serenity, humility, kindness, benevolence, empathy, generosity, truth, compassion, and faith. The same fight is going on inside you — and inside every other person too."

The grandson thought about it for a minute and then asked his grandfather, "Which wolf will win?" The elder Cherokee simply replied. "The one you feed."

Your *You* has an infinite number of faces it will present to you. Learning to track the essence of your *You*, the energetic quality it represents, will help you to see when it is at play in your life. Your mind may try to convince you that you know what is going on, that you've figured it out. Just when you think the ego is quiet it rises in a new form or in a new way. Your ego has a thousand reflections. It will shift and adapt to any situation and you'll find you are back in the thick of things without realizing how.

This is what makes energetic processes so important in awakening. The mind is infinitely tricky and loves to convince and persuade. You can repeat affirming platitudes about your awakening, but they can be masking your *You* even if they sound spiritual. You will never master your *You* by meeting it head on.

Knowing the Voice of the Soul

The soul voice within is quieter. This is why it takes time and particular movements of release for the voice of your soul to come forward. Your *You* likes to build up more of something and that is exactly why the soul uses the cracks of life to break forth.

You will learn the soul voice for the energetics that move within and around. The soul is interested in your return home. It's one goal is to remind you of what you are and why you are here. The soul will use any means necessary to achieve this one goal. It isn't that your soul is interested in your demise. Your soul looks beyond life circumstances into the heart of you. What feels life destroying in the circumstances of your life is an opportunity for your soul to beckon you home.

You will know your soul voice for the movements that it uses. These movements are counterintuitive and require a form of release that sheds control and teaches us to allow. They are often uncomfortable at first because they are unfamiliar and disorienting. They release and relinquish, over and over. That is the landscape of the soul.

Deepak Chopra describes the soul voice within like an old penny with the brightness of the metal hidden beneath what has been dulled over time. It takes elbow grease to remove the dullness in order to reveal the brightness of the awaiting metal. The shine that has always been there, hidden beneath the life's dirt was there all along, we simply could not see it. Just because we do not immediately recognize and listen to our soul voice does not mean that it isn't there. It takes focused awareness, receptivity and practice, to shine up our soul to more readily know when it is speaking to us.

Knowing more about the soul will not help in this process—the mind wants to use information to build up and this is the landscape of your *You*. Your soul is about release and return, supporting you in accessing a wiser place within. It is a movement similar to the breath where you follow the energetic movement of release to arrive in a space of stillness that awaits you.

Yielding

The movement during this process is one of yieldedness. You may have a response to the word yieldedness for it can sound passive and succumbing. To imagine living a life from this place may feel unfathomable and anything but welcome. Why would you want to yield, become vulnerable and open to a world that doesn't have your best at heart?

What we don't yet know is that yieldedness returns us to our power specifically because it places us in our home base. We've spent so much time in our lives building up and fighting for what we think we need to survive that the movement of yielding is at its essence a foreign idea. That is why we follow the energetics. We allow the movement to carry us back home through a process that becomes a familiar rhythm. It is a movement of letting go that furthers the process of awakening in profound and tangible ways.

The markers of yielding are *softening, serenity,* and *sliding* within to *stillness*, where an emerging strength rises within you from your source. The release of yielding allows you to meet the world and your circumstances in a very different way than when you address them head-on. You may experience the movement as counterintuitive and at first, feel like it is weakness and passivity. However, a yielded way of being in the world, but not of the world, becomes the inner landscape that holds you and the one you meet in living reciprocity. Be within to feel your center and to feel these movements. Your sense awareness will be your guide.

. . .

Softening

The process of softening is a relaxing motion within your body as you loosen your gaze upon the world. So often we harden ourselves to meet the challenges around us. To soften is counterintuitive. If you feel this difference within your body, one movement creates a steeling of the self. The energetic is one of hardening, of rising up, and a moving out of yourself in anticipation of what you will need to meet. Try softening now by relaxing your gaze, opening your vision, and widening your view. Feel how your body naturally responds and resets you.

Progressive muscle relaxation (PMR) is an anxiety-reduction technique first introduced by American physician Edmund Jacobson in the 1930s. It is a technique that creates a muscle memory of what it means to soften. In progressive muscle relaxation, you tense a group of muscles as you breathe in, and you relax them as you breathe out. You work on your muscle groups in a certain order. If you practice this technique correctly, you may even end up falling asleep. The purpose of the technique is that you begin to notice what a relaxed muscle feels like versus a tightened one. It is the same with softening. We slowly begin to notice what it feels like to feel the pillowy folds of our body and our energy when we are in receptivity.

The energetics of softening create a greater receptivity, where your edges soften and you relax inward. It can often feel like you are resting backward in a downward motion like settling into an overstuffed easy chair. Your gaze softens around the edges and your breath begins to quiet. There is an alertness in this position, but it doesn't have the edge and force that bracing yourself entails. This energetic movement is a readying release in order for you to receive— all of your inner channels are then available to allow what is rising to emerge.

. . .

Serenity

Our minds make assessments about what is in our best interest and they attempt to orchestrate our circumstances to match these constructs. Serenity is a movement that allows everything to simply be what it is. Serenity describes the state of allowing. As we rest more fully within this space, a wisdom and an energetic movement opens into opportunity and forward motion.

We seldom realize that our assessments and judgments actually end up creating what we don't want. Anything we bring resistance to—even through the force of our good ideas and intentions about what is best—can inadvertently create more of what is unwanted. As we learn to track the energetic movements of allowing all to be as it is, something beyond the mind is freed and begins to guide us.

There is a Zen story that describes a student who sought out the wisdom of a Buddhist monk. Many Zen stories are fictitious. This one is true.

A man went to a Buddhist monastery for a silent retreat. After he finished his retreat in silence, he felt better—calmer and stronger—but something was missing. The teacher said he could talk to one of the monks before he left. The man thought for a while, then asked: "How do you find peace?" The monk said: "I say yes. To everything that happens, I say yes." When the man returned home, he was enlightened.

The man was Kamal Ravikant. Upon returning home, he was interviewed about his experience and said in response, "Most of our pain, most of our suffering comes from resistance to what is. Life is. And when we resist what life is, we suffer. When you can say yes to life, surrender to life and say: 'Okay, what should I be now?' That's where power comes from."

By learning to simply allow everything to be as it is in the moment—the pain of the loss, the rising anxiety within our body, the sense of joy welling within—we are present within the moment and as a consequence we are within something larger that creates movement beyond the mind. By being within the now, allowing serenity in everything, we open to what we most want even if we don't yet know it.

Sliding

Softening is a readying within, and serenity a positioning of allowance that opens space for you to follow the present energies within. Sliding is a description of how it feels to follow the movement, which is similar to a downward exhale that you follow from within. It becomes more than an exhale, for the energetic movement will continue beyond the breath and will become more and more tangible as you practice sliding down deeper within. You can feel it now if you soften your positioning into serenity and follow the natural energetic movement that carries you down. Your breath can help you to follow this sliding motion from your head down into your pelvis and resting you within the awaiting silence, a placement.

The rise of virtual reality technology speaks to this feeling of sliding into an inner location. Called sensory immersion, virtual reality offers users the ability to feel 'presence'. Presence is the phenomenon a person feels when connecting to a world or environment outside of their physical body using technology as the filter. Many people describe presence not as the 'knowing' but the 'feeling' of being in a virtual space. So, too, is the phenomena of sliding into the soul state within. We enter a new landscape, one that is our true home, and our world begins to look very different.

The slide is a movement that will carry you into a position within. It will deliver you home. Learning to follow the movement is an energetic practice that you will be within more and more as you go about every task in your day. You will begin to notice when you brace yourself to meet the world with force or respond to something coming toward you. As you soften and allow all to be as it is in serenity—even if it is unwanted—you follow the energetic slide as a movement that carries you home within stillness.

Stillness

There is an awaiting quiet within you that over time will become your internal set point. For now, it is simply a space you drop within and begin to feel. It is the quiet of no-thing where the stillness envelopes. This terrain is silent without thoughts of the mind and without an awareness of self as a distinct entity.

Stillness is often likened to the quality of a large, smooth lake surface where there is no wind to create a visible current or ripple. Like a plane of glass that is smooth and unending, stillness can feel like it goes on forever. It carries a timeless, spaceless quality. Perhaps you have been out on the ocean where you could not see a horizon or the shore. You are within a vast space where even the sense of earth and sky are absent. This is how the everlasting, seamless nature of stillness feels in our physical world.

There is a quality to the stillness within for it is your home. It also becomes the starting place for opening to the wiser guidance within and around you. Without access to stillness within much of the spiritual guidance that you will give or receive will be more of the *You* than the soul. We learn to drop into and inhabit the space of stillness and await, in no-thing, what will begin to come forth

Strength

It is from here that your true strength arises. For when

you are disentangled from circumstance, you move out of illusion—what you think is real and required of you— and move more deeply into the truth of what you are. As the illusions fall away, illumination can fill you and allow active engagement with the person or situation while being fully present and unentangled at the surface. This doesn't mean you won't suffer or that life isn't challenging, rather, you'll see what is happening from a different place and meet it from the yielded position of the divine within. This is true strength, where you abide within fullness and allow life to move you from within your soul center.

In Japanese medical and martial arts traditions, the hara is a technical term for a specific area often called the belly. This belly is not the physical organ but an energy field indicative of one's true nature. According to the Aikido tradition, when the mind hara (at the head) and the earth hara (at the navel) are combined great power is actualized. Our minds are not enough to achieve power strength. In martial arts the hara is the center of our energy, the center of gravity and the location from which personal strength rises. In short, it helps us find the "guts" to be present to our life with presence, courage, and clarity.

The movements of *softening, serenity, sliding,* and *strength* become the pathway for allowing yieldedness to guide you into your deeper truth where you realize in an embodied, experiential way that peace is present at all times. Over time your body will have a visceral sense of these movements and will carry you when life is challenging or overwhelming.

Living Within Yieldedness

We know yieldedness in our own lives, both as an energetic movement within and a repositioning. When life gets challenging we are reminded to be in our sacred centers, allowing softening, serenity, and the sliding that permits all to be as it is, moving us into our true strength. This is a practice and a way of living in the world. The movement will carry you naturally when you access it without having to use the language that we suggest or name. It is the inner movement that carries you into stillness and that is the place of position for true strength within.

We realize that it can sound insurmountable to stay within this movement, especially when life feels difficult. The mind is quick to judge and assess life outcomes and it can be easy to slip out of the moment and rise into an old story about who and what you are. It may seem naive to look at the pile of bills on your counter or enter the hospital room with your loved one and stay within yieldedness. And yet, this is the returning movement that places you in the space of your soul, even when life is most challenging.

Life from within the inner depths begins to carry you along, almost under the surface, without circumstances dictating what and how things are. The movement of yieldedness is the process of allowing without expectation where life is lived more and more from the stillness within. We notice the places where our intention and resistance create and we can use the pathway of yieldedness to return to divine union within.

To expect life to be smooth sailing without suffering and struggle is unrealistic. To live this bodied existence in a soulful way is the path. Struggles are part of life and it is in noticing the toss and tumble that we get clearer about the two worlds. Yielding is the pathway into your divine center and becomes your second breath as you still, allow, and yield.

Loving the Ego

From within this developing movement we learn to distinguish our *You* from the soul, not resisting or demanding that our *You* retreat. Rather, we bring the same softening, serenity, slide and stillness to our engagement with our *You* as we do in meeting the situations of the world. We embody a space of love and allowing for when your *You* is met in this way it relaxes and begins to fall away naturally.

Ego Death?

Many traditions teach ego death where the goal is the eradication of the ego—your *You*—getting rid of it once and for all. The ego isn't all bad. It helps us navigate the tasks of life that require thinking and planning. However, the problem arises when the ego leads and there isn't any room for the soul to speak; it narrows experiencing and cuts us off from our truth. It's important to note that staying in the world, but not of the world, is what is necessary for our time in history. Those who have no ego left don't function well in daily life. They either need to retreat from everyday life or to gather a community around them to attend to tasks so that they can reside fully in the expansive consciousness of the soul.

The ego wants to be befriended. Inherent to its existence, it desires to be embraced and loved along the way. Not to be given power or authority, but rather to be given a place. Once it finds its place, it lays down, becomes as quiet as a lamb, who will give bleets at times when danger rises. But, generally, it finds that it can be content in its own place or time and that it does not need to rule or control our life any longer. How do we find this place for our ego to rest?

It is only through loving it as it rises and loving it as it lays down. It is through finding and meeting it with compassion, humor, love, joy and gratitude, that our ego, over time, knows that it will not be threatened into non-existence. Rather we can tell it that we are finding a place for it, a home for it, a position for it in our lives, and it is no longer our place of authority or wisdom or center. It, too, will go gently, and it will find its place of home, and it will be at peace.

With Love

Energetic Awakening allows everything and helps you relate in love to the ego *You*. This is a distinctive in energetic awakening—that your *You* is valued for what it is meant to do and guided away from terrain that does not belong to it. This is the illusion that great teachers speak about when they name that as the ego falls away true life can be lived. The path of love allows us to honor its role without getting attached. As we notice the two voices more and more, a natural separation occurs and it is this opening that allows you to quiet the *You's* persistent voice and create space for the soul.

This process follows yieldedness in addressing the ego as well as your life. The movement is one of love and you meet your *You* with the same softening and serenity that we bring through yieldedness, allowing it to quiet and find its rightful place within. For, the ego does have a place in our life, one that is tremendously important if you choose to stay engaged in the world. Remember, your ego is what helps you stay within the world, buying groceries and doing laundry.

Thinning of Your *You*

We found an immense sense of relief as our egos began to quiet. There was a palpable, "Oh, thank you. I don't have to carry all of this any longer." For the ego loves to carry and hold and keep and take care of. The freedom born of love was unmistakable. To love our fragile ego selves meant it no longer needed to be the vantage point from which we viewed the world. The soul took this place where there was only silence and allowed all to be as it is.

This is where the ego begins to shift and life begins to alter. This is a pathway of detachment where the ego *You* and how the ego understands and defines itself in relationship to what is 'other,' those people, places and things that it used to seek meaning from, through its connection melts away. Rather, it simply lays down because that which it is most attached to begins to fall away. There is nothing there to connect to anymore. This process involves loss and pain, and it is also an opportunity for gratitude and joy, for what was once considered a source of happiness alters when it is no longer attached to the people, places and things that it used to be located in.

As what you once called *You* begins to thin, your soul becomes the lens through which you view the world. You are within a new consciousness and from here you come alongside your *You* with love. This process is less about overcoming and more about gentling. It is through great love for what we have built over our lifetime that we begin to slip into the essence of the soul.

This new consciousness is finding a way to bring the ego alongside our spiritual process, not for its obliteration or its demise, but so that it too may find its true home in our familiar state. In this way it can connect back into its own true nature. It becomes a way to navigate and function but it is no longer the primary location within.

Energetic Experiencing

There is a chatter within that is ready to be released. Its fatiguing monologue is primed to suspend and be placed back into its rightful place. For long this voice has been a comforting companion, and the partnership is reordering into how it all began. The voice deep within you that saw the world as light is rising. It's an enduring voice within you. This chatter you have known is constructed. Yet, there is no need to say goodbye. The change is the most natural one in the world, one of ease. It is putting your inner life back into a permanent divine order. Your wisdom is speaking. Listen and lean into it and the order will follow.

1. **Center:** By now you know that to center is to come home. Find this positioning now and you may notice that it is easier and easier to drop within at a moment's notice. Even at the split second of centering, there may be a quickening voice that emerges. Notice it. It may feel like a wobble or tightening. All is the resistance of your *You* emerging in the very moment that you detach and center. The sacred division is creating the delineation that allows for sacred re-ordering.
2. **Release**: As you feel the quickening movement of restriction, there is the pivot point of tightening against or leaning with love into. Soften and slide deeper. Resistance when met head on will increase. Lightly touch into your *You* with gentle feather-light presence of love. Follow how it responds from within the experience. You may feel a many-directed movement of letting go for it is what we love that we also release. Your ego is quieting. Laying down into a slumber. Not gone forever but happily settling into its place.
3. **Receive**: A second movement will follow. For a period of time you may feel space and silence. Absolutely nothing. Over time it is the silence that will bring forward the something you have been aching for. To push in the silence and demand its communication will bring forward

greater silence and rouse the ego from its slumber. Stay in the stillness. Embrace the silence. Open into the space. It is the ground of being from which the soul will speak. You may begin to sense a rising energy. It may be words, an image, a sense, a sound, or that which you cannot even describe. But it still carries the vibration of the stillness that is only present in the thinning of your *You*. This awareness within is your soul. Like a voice that is familiar yet a distant echo, it rises to meet you.

This voice is not new. Remember that you need not search for it. If you are searching or striving, it is your *You* telling you that you cannot find the soul without effort. Like a love who has been eagerly awaiting your return, with intention and awareness, that soul will rise with ease and welcome you. Over time you will learn to differentiate your *You* voice from your soul. Distinguishing between the two can only emerge from positioning within. Your *You* is a master of disguise and chasing it is futile. When you come home within, there is no chase or pinning down the ever-changing face of your ego. Instead you will begin to know it vibrationally. There is a feeling slightly out of yourself when you are in the ego. To land firmly within the soul, this is your guide. Lean into the stillness within the soul. And when you feel out, come back in. It is that simple. From this place, the separation between the two will continue.

5

NAVIGATING BETWEEN WORLDS

Meister Eckhart (1260-1327) was a German theologian, philosopher and mystic who famously said, "Theologians may quarrel but the mystics of the world speak the same language." His works have become a common language, a foundation for many modern spiritual understandings from Zen Buddhism to contemplative Christianity. From his mystical experiences he described four main stages of union between the soul and Divine: dissimilarity, similarity, identity and breakthrough. Specifically, in the stage of similarity we understand ourselves as in our fullness or in union with the Divine.

He is known for his pithy sayings and his play on words, a trait that led to his becoming a subject of a great inquisition. His writings often prompt his readers (past and present) to pause and scratch their heads in wonder. He invites us into a place of inquiry and wonder between the world we know through the You and the world we are living into in the Soul. Some of his most famous plays on words include:

"The eye through which I see God is the same eye through which God sees me; my eye and God's eye are one eye, one seeing, one knowing, one love."

"Only the hand that erases can write the true thing."

"Truly, it is in the darkness that one finds the light, so when we are in sorrow, then this light is nearest of all to us."

"I am what I wanted and I want what I am."

"When the Soul wants to experience something she throws out an image in front of her and then steps into it."

Even now can you feel how his words bridge a space between what the worlds of what we know of our You and what we are returning to of our Soul? We navigate between being similar and dissimilar in the journey from the You to the soul until we finally land in the familiar soul forever.

You may be able to reflect on it now—the way you feel in relationship to the circumstances of your life. The voice of your soul is speaking more often and this is shifting life in the ordinary and also within the deeper reflective places. A hum is developing—an energetic awareness—that pulses rhythmically within you. It reminds you to attend differently in the spaces of intentional reflection and retreat and also in the ordinary events of your life.

Walking Between Worlds

It may feel like you are living in two distinct places, a world of the ordinary and an emerging space of quiet within. You do the things you perceive must be done—working, tending family, maintaining the lifestyle you've created—while periodically dropping into a different space of connection and increasing silence. The movement may be within your awareness or it may simply be carrying you back and forth.

This season is marked by this movement— moving from your outer world into your inner world. You are becoming comfortable with a flow that is helping you whether you recognize it or not. The rhythm is a form of acclimation that opens and moves you, helping you to calibrate to something new. Ordinary life meeting soul and soul meeting ordinary life. As they move back and forth there is also a space in-between that is weaving itself together. Like a conversation between new friends there is a period of acclimation and calibration before a comfort settles in.

Following Life's Streams

Life becomes like a stream. If you imagine a stream from different vantage points you will feel its movement and how this relates to your life now. The stream helps to experientially imagine the feeling from each unique perspective.

Life Circumstances

Watching from the stream's edge you may perceive the constant movement as the water gurgles and bubbles, swirls and ripples. Various impediments and alterations in the terrain impact how the water flows. A large boulder in the middle creates a damming and pressure and the water must find its way around. Twists and bends in the stream create ripples and whirlpools of swirling water and when it runs free it can look as smooth as glass.

This image mirrors life looked at from the edge. So often we relate only to our circumstances, the boulders, twists and turns or free flowing periods, for how our life is going. Standing at the edge of life and looking directly at it, that is simply what you see.

Up until this point you have related to life in this way. From where you were standing—how you were positioned—influenced the perspective that you carried. For most of us, we've never even considered another way of looking. All of our energy is spent in working with the currents— the stories and events that are influencing our life. Most of us want water that runs smooth and free so we spend our energy attempting to make this happen. Whether it is more free because of time on the weekends, a better paying job, a different spouse, we put all of our energy into moving and adjusting the boulders and debris.

Efforting to Make Change

What many of us now realize is that the impediments never end. The circumstances and situations that influence the river will always and forever continue. Just when you think you've got it made—you have received the promotion or the divorce is final—down comes an uprooted tree crashing into your now calmed life stream and the waters again can no longer flow freely.

Even our attempts to heal the pain of these impediments becomes consuming. We invest tremendous resources and life energy in shifting the terrain. A beautiful part of this process is that some things really do transform. Our lives can get much, much better. We get rid of what is not in our highest good to allow something new to flow. We can also get stuck in looking at the problems and expending all of our energy in trying to shift the terrain and get bogged down in the process.

Something else can happen in this process, often out of awareness and unnamed. Your relationship to the stream can alter. Looking back you notice that the boulders just don't bother you in the same way and the newly fallen tree isn't as disruptive as you thought. You may find yourself stepping into the cool waters and enjoying them even though the initial cold gave a sting. The landscape isn't altering that much but your relationship to it is. And, this is the magic. You begin to feel different in your surroundings, within your own skin, and the world begins to shift. The river looks and feels different as you step within it. You begin to directly connect with the waters in a new way where you don't look at them, you connect to them from within.

All of the cracks and falling away have allowed you to

step into the waters and tolerate the unwanted phenomena of life. Tolerating the mess has allowed you to simply be within and notice your surroundings in a new way. The rising soul voice has your attention just a bit more. You can see and begin to feel your life's stream in a slightly different way. What once was story and circumstance has altered and a space has been made for you to get in and begin to feel from a very different place and in a very new way.

Dropping Within

You are entering the waters of your life. Instead of looking at life from the outside, a place is being created for you to drop into something deeper, more essential, about what you are. You've needed time to get here, for without some sparks to prompt you and some tolerance for the disorder that the cracks of life have created, you would have stayed out and never gotten in. All of your energy would have compelled you to remain on the edge of your life looking in. And from that perspective all you see is your circumstances and the stories they connect to.

Your recognition of your soul voice is prompting a new awareness and a new willingness. You are hearing the distinction between your *You* and your soul and tracking the movement of energy by being in your Centers within the everyday—especially when life rocks you. This increasing awareness is showing you that there is something below the surface waters of your life. You may be sensing this at the edges of your experience that there is an inner world within your skin of the surface that awaits you. Knowing that you are more than your bodied existence and feeling the settledness with your heart and wisdom centers increases this awareness more and more.

You can feel just a bit more that you are within something. No longer are you looking at life, you are the experiencer from within what is emerging. You are becoming part of the water that carries the stream.

It can be shocking at first, the moment you sink below a body of water down from the visible world above and into the silence just below the surface. When you naturally allow this release, a whole new world opens. The quiet is enveloping. The water hugs around you like a buoyant blanket and holds you within something radically different from the surface waters above. If you've ever sunk down in a swimming pool filled with laughing children or allowed your body to drop below the waves of the ocean, you know this feeling. You enter another world of silence that is not only quiet, but shockingly calm. The waves can crash above you, but the currents—the energy—simply rocks and moves you within its embrace.

The popular meditation application called *Insight Timer* has its own series of underwater meditations to induce the feeling of being submerged. The meditations evoke the deep feeling of being at the ocean's depths. In a blog post connected to these meditations, Janette Freeman describes the powerful qualities of being beneath the surface. She writes, "With the sounds and distractions of the world drowned out, you become so much more aware of the unique sounds of the ocean, waves breaking in the distance, boat motors overhead, currents moving, but most of all your own breathing. Listening to what is around you takes you even deeper into peace— in life and under the sea."

It can feel frightening at first to let your body sink and to trust that you are held by this enveloping space. Even if you don't swim, you may know spaces where a quiet that is complete begins to surround you—the dark of night or the calm of a peaceful landscape— and you feel enveloped in something larger than simple silence. This is like the space of your inner depths. You are entering a landscape within (and surrounding you) that is still and quiet no matter what is happening around you. It isn't a one dimensional quiet, but rather a stillness that opens into something much larger and vastly rich in its connecting.

It takes time to become acclimated to the still waters. The inner depths are still, quiet, tranquil. They are also darker and less activated for they do not relate to circumstances and happenings like what occurs up above. At first it can feel lonely and foreign. Your instinct may be to feel it very quickly and then rise back out. Or to create some of your own waves or ripples. In this process you are sinking more deeply into your inner experiencing as this new awareness holds you.

You may even notice that the space between the surface and the depths has its own push and pull as you move back and forth. You may have an emerging sense of the space between the surface and the deeper inner waters with some tangible, visceral internal markers. The surface moves you and you are in relationship to what is happening up there. The moment you strive to live from this familiar state, efforting and trying, the greater the surface ripples, growing stronger and stronger for your efforting—for whatever you attend to and attempt to shift with force grows larger.

We often want to move beyond what is uncomfortable. Becoming familiar with the surface and the depths takes time. Many forge ahead and work to sink themselves more quickly to hurry a process that just takes time. It may feel clumsy and like you are failing in some way. There is no achievement or timeline to follow. Openness and awareness are your guides and the process of allowing your rhythm, over and over again.

The only choice, other than stirring and living at the surface to stay connected to circumstances, is to slip in more deeply and allow the water to carry you in your inward descent. For the more you reside within the still waters the more familiar they become and the more noticeable when you are not there. You are within experience as you allow and your soul will carry you deeper into your truth as you allow the deepening to live fully within you.

Phil Jackson won 11 NBA Championship rings for his role as a basketball coach—six wins with the Chicago Bulls and five with the LA Lakers. He is the most successful coach not only in NBA history, but in the history of professional sports the world over.

Raised in a Penecostal home and molded from a young age to be a minister, Phil lived in a world without TV, movies, and limited contact with broader influences. He did play basketball and he was good at it and this eventually led him to a successful coaching career where he was known not only for his strategy, but also for his character.

Phil regularly worked with well-formed egos. He is known for finding a way for Kobe Bryant, Shaq, Scottie Pippen, Michael Jordan and others to align their skill on behalf of the whole team. He is widely known for using a soulful approach to coaching alongside skill, aptitude, and analytics. In his own words, he says:

"After years of experimenting, I discovered that the more I tried to exert power directly, the less powerful I became. I learned to dial back my ego and distribute power as widely as possible without surrendering final authority."

Perhaps Phil's story is an example of rising to the surfaces of these waters when the moment calls for a clear play of action in a tight game. Yet, the depth of his character— the soulful quality with which he coached— was what truly guided his many teams to victory after victory after victory. A quietly placed ego shines when aligned with the leadership of the soul.

It simply requires dropping into this space every now and again, noticing how you rise to the surface and descend again, back and forth as what you refer to as *You* sinks more deeply into the truth of what you are. You often don't know what is happening. You are simply responding to the ascent and descent of life—a moment of stillness in a busy, fast paced schedule, a glistening leaf that catches the sun at the breaking of dawn, an awareness of something larger that surrounds you as you make dinner for the seventh time this week. They show up and submerge you—without any awareness of how to integrate them—you are simply in the experience as it rises.

Inhabiting the Depths

You will know the waters of the soul by how they feel. There is no way to bypass this knowing. For if you wish to go into this space via the mind you can't. You are no longer within the thinking mind. It is no longer available to you.

The depths of the soul are primarily marked by an unshakable sense of peace and stillness that goes beyond reason. It is a state of being within where you actually dwell within—your soul waters— and it may feel like the rest of the world goes silent. The silence can feel so loud it is deafening. You are learning to live separated and detached from your circumstances. You are within complete stillness.

Like the movement downward as you submerge yourself underwater, there is a sense of another world that you are entering that is devoid of stimuli or perception. You are experiencing the sense of void or no-thing that is part of the soul. You know that the soul exists because it is. There is nothing that is dependent on it or an exterior circumstance or perception that makes it real. This is the suspended space that opens in these quiet depths. No time, no space, no-thing. There is only an ineffable quality of complete and utter stillness. There is delight in resting in this location, for your whole existence has been to find this place. The world goes silent and there is no need for anything any longer.

You can slowly see how you have been turning toward

this location from the moment the spark began and there is a desire to stay in this location of comfort and the silence that transcends the ears and lives on forever. You are within your true home as you abide here more and more.

Ripples

Your growing awareness of these two voices makes you encounter life differently and the people gathered around you will begin to notice. The movement at your surface begins to ripple outward into your surrounding world and it feels like you don't have much control over how you impact the world around you.

We realized that this period is where we got edgy and reactive, sometimes while we were trying our hardest to hold it together and be spiritual. It's as if any construction that is built with effort on the identity of the *You* is up for grabs and life has a way of undoing it for you. If you lived with us, you might have seen some erratic behavior and volatile reactions as we faced the growing conversation within and without. There is nothing to fall back on, especially not social graces, and at the end of the day you may feel yourself taking one long deep sigh as you scan the events that unfolded.

In this period in our lives, we found ourselves clinging to what we knew to be secure as though our lives depended on it. And it did. We knew there was a slipping release and we clawed toward what was secure in the most nonsensical ways. From immense effort into incidental events or intently narrowing in on what used to be off-the-cuff, there was a latching on before a letting go. There were times when we began to feel disoriented and we reached outside of ourselves in order to bring a false sense of orientation. What we didn't yet know is that the reorientation was truly found within.

While all of this can lead to a feeling of disorientation, it is movement. If you can love this time of disorientation, the movement will carry you deeper inward to your truth. If you allow yourself to experience the ride that is carrying you, there is less resistance and when there is less resistance things tend to smooth on their own. Expect to feel a bit lost and assume you will grapple with life to regain or re-find a sense of location within one self. Allow love to guide you, for that is what is most needed during this season, in order to live into this process, not bypass it. Not love with an aim or a goal. Simply love for love's sake, for that is the space you are awakening within.

What we slowly became aware of is that our well-oriented lives were illusions. The security that lay quietly as ground beneath our feet wasn't our truth and the disorienting moments became re-orienting. And the pendulum swing became less -or maybe it was our minds that created this movement. As the mind released, there was less perceived vacillation. What the mind called secure was no longer stable. What the mind called routine was not stabilizing. What the mind called upended was not upside down but right side up.

Pendulum Swing

It is important to know that the sense of *You* may rise more strongly during this period as the *You* separates from the soul. Your *You* wants desperately to regain the ground that it perceives is being lost. You may experience these swings like a pendulum moving back and forth within you. First you swing to one side experiencing yourself in a state of integration, wholeness, and clarity where you feel the authenticity of engaging the world from the place of soul. And then life swings you to the other side where you give an opposite response only a moment later. The swing is a force that carries you and it rises without awareness. You may experience your *You* lashing out, becoming territorial, seeking to preserve the created individual identity that you have developed. It may come across as selfish or reactionary. The ego, *You*, simply wants to preserve what has been established. It is self-preservation against the tidal movement that is growing within you.

The Paradox

Even in the midst of the pendulum swing, bubbles are emerging from your water's deep as the soul rises into your awareness and you allow life to no longer fit. You now know that you are living within a paradox as the separation between the *You* and the soul continues without anything tangible to fill the empty spaces. What was once tightly bound and neatly organized unwinds and you enter a season of disorientation.

You may experience a rubber band snap-back after a period of expansion where initially there is the bliss of experiencing a sense of joy and love that is from "no-thing" or without attachment followed by the *You's* response to the expansion that snaps us back into illusion. This movement, even if discouraging, is one of deepening and descent. Your *You* will frame it as "failure" or "being on the wrong path" but, your ego state is not the lens in which to view your descent any more. The *You* is inherently dualistic in that it wishes to characterize a spiritual experience as a method of regaining control. The bliss state of love without attachment that you begin to experience in these pendulum swings is also your greatest ally.

As you love all that is you find an expanse of Divine love emerging for the totality of spiritual descent and move beyond the responses of pain that emerge within the movement and countermovement, for they are simply circumstances and nothing more.

Between Two Worlds

As the *You* and the soul begin to separate more and more, moments will arise where you no longer fit within the life you have created. No longer do you have access to dipping down into your depths and rising to the surface to live from the *You* to keep your life humming along. Life begins to feel somewhat off kilter and the dissonance becomes increasingly jarring. Most often, these moments arrive in the most routine of experiences. You may be sitting in the car going to work, attending a meeting, or gathering at the annual family event and you notice that something isn't quite as easy as it used to be. These moments come as flashes at first —moments that signal that something isn't quite right—and you feel the lack of fit and the sense of immanent disintegration of what was.

This is a key: what was once an integrated whole is beginning to separate within you. You can feel like life is bifurcated, cut in two. You may go to an event or work function and you can do the chit chat and chatter that is necessary for social graces, and yet that deeper state is always calling you, beckoning you to find it as your source and your center.

At times it can feel like living in two worlds. You notice your higher self or your soul rising in small moments where you experience a point of clarity or you find a response within that feels very different than the way you would have ordinarily responded. Perhaps it comes in the form of an argument or a moment of tension with someone where the retort that you may have made no longer slips easily off your tongue. Instead, there is a pause where you find that it is not as easy to interact in the way that you once did.

As the Soul and the *You* separate more and more, there is a point where you intentionally live as if there are two planes of existence—two different places that you live within. On the one hand you are still living in the state of *You*— fully aware of the identities and the self that you have built over years—and you are also aware of your deeper soul state that is holding you, calling you.

It can feel like you now live in two places or on two levels—one is the bubbles and ripples at the surface of the water where your *You* engages and reacts to all of the currents that are moving you and one where you rest down deep below the currents of life within your deeper soul state. With each passing day and in every breath you walk these two planes of awareness and simply notice.

At this point, even though you still experience the two states as bifurcated and separate, you are able to travel back and forth with greater ease. You have more volition to drop down and abide and you notice the currents when you rise up. This is a marker to notice along the way. This can become a reference point for you that you are able to shift into a higher consciousness, moving into your higher self, allowing you to shift more easily out of your *You* state into your soul essence—at least for a period of time. For, even though you have more capacity to notice and shift, you continue to return back to your sense of location, who you are, in your *You*.

This season lasted for what felt like a long time. We noticed the distinctness of the two worlds. We were still fully planted within the world we were living in without major disruptions to the actual tasks that we were involved in. And yet, we were in them differently—at least some of the time. Rhythms such as walking in the early morning and listening more broadly from within an emerging silence were significant for us. They weren't the practices that we had adopted over years of training that involved strategies or systems. It was more of a soulful sense that infused every day compelling us out and in. We noticed that for once we weren't efforting. There was a larger awakening movement guiding us.

Sometimes you must give up your daily practices for they can be of the mind and the construction of your *You*. Our systems can become our stumbling blocks because of their ordered demands. That is why an energetic movement is offered for you to follow over and over again. Allowing and releasing is our lifebreath.

It might be that moment where you do speak and instantly it feels off, not right, because it has the vibration of the *You*. You realize from within that you can't engage in the same way anymore. A quietness is present where more words might have otherwise been and you have a glimmer of a different way that is emerging.

Thomas Merton is arguably the most influential American Catholic author of the twentieth century. His autobiography, *The Seven Storey Mountain*, has sold over one million copies and he wrote over sixty other books and hundreds of poems and articles on topics ranging from monastic spirituality to civil rights, nonviolence, and the nuclear arms race. He also struggled with depression and anxiety. He yearned for complete contemplative solitude and often felt in the wrong place, like "a duck in a chicken coop,"and sought to secure a full-time hermitage for his solitude. He finally secured a hermitage on a hilled, wooded area and proclaimed himself unencumbered from monastery life and interfering monks. Story has it that he prompted and definitively walked up to his hermitage on Mount Olivet. After only a week, word trickled back to the monastery that he had complained that no one had made any efforts to find out how he was getting on.

This small anecdote about Thomas Merton illumines that while we attune to the silent solitude of the soul, the *You* still rises often and regularly, it wonders and checks in with the outside world. We never fully arrive in a place in which our *You* is not present in the form of a depression, a loneliness, a flash of bitterness. It is the very meaning of being human.

You are beginning to tune into life and increase awareness about unseen spaces by resting more deeply within the soul waters, at least every now and again. Remember, this process is leading you and you are not in control of it. The movement is as much a marker as the content, for that is part of the deepening.

The richness that arrives from within this landscape is almost unspeakable. When accessed, there is a sweetness and wordless wonder about this space of stillness. In times past we would wonder how mystics and saints could sit in silence for long periods of time and feel that anything of significance was happening. The assumption is that the place must be nothing, vacancy. And, yes, part of that is true, but within the silence everything exists. Words no longer need to be exchanged in the same way for one just knows from within what is deeply connected in dirt, tree, voice, sky, star, spirit, laundry. As you allow the movement of yielding to carry you more deeply inward you realize that everything is animate and infused from your inhabiting in the deep waters of the soul. It takes no effort. Only presence.

Energetic Experiencing

To drop into the quiet depths of the soul is to follow an energetic movement. You know how to drop into the heart center and wisdom center and there are passageways in each that locate you fully in the soul. Do not think too hard about this. For if you try to find these passageways, they will not be there. It is in making space and hollowing out within that these passageways into the quiet depths that await you will appear. When we pass through the narrow point of nothing (the void) we open into the soul. This is because the *You* cannot accompany you into the vastness of the soul. There is an aspect in this passageway in which your *You* truly separates in order to drop into these depths. Do not bypass this experience. It is in the releasing that you are set free to submerge into these waters.

1. **Center:** Find your positioning. Already you are beginning the separation process. You will become familiar with the immediate twinge of the *You's* protest. Love it for what it is. It will quiet. Drop fully within your heart center. Travel deeper into your wisdom center. Stay within both centers and notice that there is movement. It may feel like a clearing or an opening as emotion, story, and circumstance are shifting. It may feel like an eternity of staying present. And yet, you stay where you are.
2. **Opening**: You will notice a small opening beginning. Like a small pinpoint of light or the clearing that breaks open as fog dissipates, this is the movement of a passageway. This may be felt in your body. You may sense outside of you or within you. There is no right way to follow an opening but it is a threshold for you of crossing over into the location of the soul. As you feel an opening emerging, there is no need to figure it out. You will not know where you are going. If you do know, it is your ego.
3. **Follow:** Follow the opening that is presenting itself to you. As you move into it you may feel some rising fear. This is the narrowing in which the ego cannot cross over. Your *You* will resist the movement. Practice love and acceptance. Continue to move as you may feel like it is one

step at a time, one breath at a time, one moment at a time. You will know the rightness of the experience by the movement. There is a consistency to the opening that will persevere. Stay within, move with, follow. You will experience landing motion at some point in time. It may be now or later. It does not matter. When you land in the soul, you know it. The peace and stillness is unique in that you cannot find it in our physical world. It is also marked by no thing or no form. Immerse yourself in this stillness. Welcome home.

When you find yourself migrating to the surfaces in life, do not worry. These depths are available for you anytime and anywhere. You may feel frustration, and while there is still a migratory pattern in between, this is necessary for you to stay awake in everything. For what you are moving toward is a full integration in which you live from these depths. At this moment, though, it is the movement in between the *You* and the soul that is showing you their separation. It is from knowing polarities that union can emerge. So, when you are in the soul's depths, bask in its encompassing embrace. When you find yourself bobbing to the surface, accept that it is as it is. This movement alone will keep you diving deep time and time again.

6

RISING WORLDS THAT MEET YOU

St Francis of Assisi was familiar with the work of the earth and the work of the material world. As the son of a cloth merchant, he worked in the material world in the bartering and exchanging of goods. In 1202 he marched off to battle in Perugia and was taken prisoner. After being ransomed, he lived a year of convalescence after a long illness in which he received visions and dreams to "go repair my house which has fallen in ruin." From this message, he took up an itinerant life with the commitment to live, not without possessions, but without possessing. Thus, his work changed. No longer did his work involve the material world. His work was of the earth.

This change of heart is not idyllic or bucolic. It isn't what we make him out to be. Francis of Assisi was a nature mystic. He spoke with fire and laughed with wind. As he traveled and gathered his followers, his messages were ones of religious revival and repentance. The wild-eyed mystic called for a change of heart in the affluent and indifferent. As he lived the itinerant life, all of nature was his teacher about the infinite love of God. Each flower pointed toward Divine love. Each vast field opened him into a larger relationship with the greatest love. It was a relationship of sacred reciprocity. The natural world was not a stepping stone in order to ascend to God. Rather, he experienced

God in every living thing, calling his beloved "Brother Wind," "Brother Fire," and "Sister Mother Earth."

A New Location Within

From this moment of emerging awareness you start to recognize that you are located more and more in your soul. No longer are you grounded in the self that you've developed over all of these years. Life lived at the surface where you define yourself by your situation and your circumstances is altered. No more are you the identities or labels that you call yourself or the people gathered around you and the landscapes surrounding you.

You are residing more regularly within your soul essence. You have access to your inner depths and they begin communicating the truth of what you are through everything. Your circumstances are not directly engaged like they once were. Yes, you are present with what is rising, but no longer do they dictate or define without reflection. You are within stillness even when the surface waters rumble and the waves begin to move. From within the landscape of the soul you are positioned differently and this spaciousness begins communicating through you.

Don't get stuck on the naming of what it is and how it shows up, for that will slow your opening. Rather, allow awareness to guide you and begin to show you how what you thought was you actually isn't and that there is something more to who and what you are that is now rising. Follow the energetic movement that you are within and let this be your guide.

Marc Parat developed a concept for a pocket crystal in 1989. While at the Aspen Institute, he heard the challenge to develop the future from Abraham Lincoln's famous saying, "the best way to predict the future is to create it." From this vision, he created a prototype for a device that would be a pocket computer, very personally focused on how we connected with others and information. As he said, "wouldn't it be great if your letters just fell out of the sky into your hand?" His prototype is the current iPhone.

When asked how he came up with this prototype, he said "there comes a moment that for some reason you are in the future and you just see it." He said that he literally stood inside of the future and just saw the phone. From this seeing, he created his prototype and the phone that we now know was visioned into reality. The connection between innovation and what has been called "spiritual seeing" is no longer separate. What the greatest of minds know is that by seeing the future, it invites us into the sacred space of co-creativity.

No longer is the unseen world only sequestered in spirituality or woo woo experience. Rather, as we learn to live in reciprocity with what is unseen, we are accessing the wisdom, insight, and guidance that is ready to be applied in our own context. You may know many stories in the world of how creation and innovation emerged from paying attention to the natural world. Or, how a mystical experience sparked research and development. It could be during a coffee break with a friend where you are fully in the moment doodling on the napkin that sparks a new idea.

When we see into the matrix of interconnection, it provides us access to a world that is ready to share the beauty of its secrets, but only in sacred reciprocity. It is paying with equal attention to what is unknown as what we know—honoring what is hidden just behind the curtain of our mind and its expectations. You may have had dreams that carried messages for you that you found oddly synchronistic when they came true. Or, it may have felt as though someone or something was with you that you couldn't see, but knew you were protected in some way. Later you then realized you evaded something catastrophic. To live is to dwell in these awakened landscapes and they are eager to live us into our fullest expression.

Withinness

You are in this moment. You are in the now. When you drop into this space you are within something larger than what the eyes can see and what the mind can conceive. To be placed fully within any given moment is where the world opens and rises within and around you. You are within and also outside of time and space. You have access to a dimensional landscape that is the phenomena that so many of us seek. It is from within this space that everything begins to open.

The key is to be within completely. Without even knowing it, we can be poised just slightly outside of any given moment looking in. Instead of releasing completely into the awaiting stillness where there is no-thing, we keep a foot on solid ground in order to observe the experiencing of what often feels like nothing. It is tremendously disorienting to drop fully within this space and simply allow. We try to keep a handhold so that we don't get lost and so we won't feel the disorientation of no self, no position, no place.

It takes time to rest within this space and to tolerate the discomfort. It can be described as an active pause where thoughts are stilled completely without any ability to reflect on what is or isn't happening. Emotions like anxiety or fear often emerge within the silence and the automatic pattern is to connect them to a story or an outcome. The practice is to return within stillness over and over again and simply abide in silence.

. . .

In a TedEd lesson, engineer Destin Sandlin demonstrates this process as he unlearned how to ride a bike. For fun, a group of his colleagues rigged a bicycle to turn right when the handlebars steered left and to turn left when the handlebars steered right. He said, once you have a rigid way of thinking in your mind, you literally do not know how to do something new. No one could ride the bike without falling off.

Destin practiced riding the bike for 5 minutes a day and it took him 8 months to ride the backwards bike. He says that if there were any distractions, like a cell phone ringing or someone calling his name, he would fall off. He had to be completely present in what was happening in order to unlearn. After mastering the backward bike, he returned and attempted to ride a regular bike and promptly fell off. However, after 20 minutes of riding the regular bike again, he was able to master both. His research and lesson speaks to the neuroplasticity of the brain and implicit bias, but also the space of neutrality that stillness and unknowing provides.

Only by suspending thought and moving into the place in which we are actively unlearning and unknowing can we experience the purity of experiencing without bias. Our mind will always put forward the predictable pathways of expectation. True guidance that is unfiltered by the mind rises only in unlearning and shifting into the present, ever expansive still state of being where we are a blank slate for wisdom to rise. As Destin notes in his summary, knowledge does not equal understanding. Understanding is born of stillness and the space of no thought.

The author of the Cloud of Unknowing is an unnamed work from the 14th century. Much of its power comes through its anonymity. To be named is the antithesis of its message. For the work points us again and again into what stillness unearths. To know what is of God is to unknow everything that we may perceive or expect to be true. Only in this state of no-thing can we glimpse even a hint of what may be Divine movement. As one translation states, "God cannot be known by reason, nor by thought, caught or sought by understanding."

To live into stillness, the place that all true guidance rises from, is only possible through the necessary process of unlearning, unknowing, no-thought, no-thing. You will ask, "What is there then?" And this is what it is all about. For unless we know how to be in the silent void in which we are absent and the silence is present, we do not experience the world without the bias of our mind.

There can be a panic in not knowing how a task will get done or whether a project will get turned in. Somehow it does. It is teaching us that there is a better way to live that is not fraught in the white-knuckled grip of the *You*. For once, you are not relying on your competence to get things done. It is a radical step of trust for the wise mind rooted in the soul to answer emails, get kids on the bus, send in payments on time and have a conversation at Thanksgiving dinner. There is always the point of tolerance in unknowing. For, it no longer works to function as you once did; however, you feel the fear from wondering how life will get done in this new paradigm.

Something From No-Thing

You will begin to rest within a space of stillness more and more, that can at first feel like nothing. It can be experienced as a place of no-thing because there isn't the stuff that we typically relate to to orient ourselves in time and space. The space you will inhabit more and more is quiet, vast, open, the true place of no-thing. No-thing is the space of stillness where you simply rest and allow. Stillness is your access point for opening to the realms within you and around you from this point forward.

This stillness is not a temporal reality of our world. Rather it is a new way of being that allows access to a dimensional space. We live into stillness and carry it with us in everything that we do and engage. Stillness is a living meditation in that the mind begins to quiet without effort. We find times of no-thought and no-emotion emerging more and more often. There is flattening of both thought and emotion, which brings about complete neutrality. We are separating from "the other" so that we can eventually be merged with it. It is when we may experience nothing in relation to what we encounter in the world that we will be merged with it in oneness. The main point is that when stillness and centeredness become our way of being, guidance emerges.

Stillness is the predicator to the collective. It is only through learning to live in complete stillness (neutrality) that we transcend our usual responses to life. This can sound like a deadening or a tuning out. It is the opposite. To reside within stillness is to allow the richness of that which is within and surrounds you without to more fully connect us with everything in an immediate and deeply tangible way.

The more you position from within stillness, the greater the opening from the place of no-thing. Through the process of yielding and allowing in the downward descent home, you open to the expanse within that holds you in quiet stillness. This is not the silence of absence, but the full presence of no-thing without attachment or effort that begins to rise within you. You drop into stillness, rest in no-thing and from within that space (one one thousand, two one thousand, three one thousand) something begins to rise within you.

Rising Worlds

The world that surrounds you—the interconnection of all things in the living matrix we call life—opens to you from this place of receptive stillness. You are met by the landscapes that we can describe as the subtle, mystical, and natural realms—the spaces that we often overlook and dismiss or relate to for our own ends rather than for our participation in the living conversation.

This is a different stance from one where you attempt to make something happen. What is referred to as spiritual guidance can come both from your ego *You* and be in service to your *You* meaning that it helps you live a better life at the surface of your circumstances. This is where guidance from the soul and guidance given from and to the ego are quite different.

Guidance that Builds Up More

Most of what comes forth in life is from the construction of the ego *You* and this informs even what we call spiritual. The guidance from the *You* can sound "spiritual" or wise, but it has a different purpose. It supports the surface aspects of your life—your circumstances and situations. It also has a distinctive vibration and tone that is distinctly different from the guidance of the soul.

In times past, divine guidance was used in a different way than it is now. Guidance can be used to build up and solidify what is of the surface realms, the space of the *You*, or it can be a deepening into the soul state within. In the awakening process the mystical realms are more about undoing than solidification as they are pointing you towards living awake. These realms can be accessed as an end in themselves. They can help the *You* (the ego) find its place in the world. The goal or focus on the mystical, natural, or subtle worlds is then a guidance and wisdom that strengthens your location in life—giving direction for greater security, greater stability, greater permanence.

Consider the story of Daniel. King Nebuchadnezzar summoned magicians, enchanters, sorcerers, and astrologers to interpret his dreams. They asked him to tell them what the dream was before answering it. This method of listening into etheric space needs something to hang on to. Classically speaking, the ego needs a foothold to go into this surrendered space. This is why many use metaphysical tools as access points into the world that is rising to meet us.

Daniel accessed the mystery of God (or etheric, cosmic space) differently. During the night, God revealed the mystery via a vision that came out of what we call the void, no-thing, complete surrender. Daniel's words are powerful. "He gives wisdom to the wise and knowledge to the discerning. He reveals deep and hidden things; he knows what lies in darkness and light dwells with him." From this positioning, God's omniscience is available to Daniel. However, it is not accessed by the ego. It is only available through the soul, which is already in union. This is why it comes at night which is symbolic of unknowing, yieldedness, mystery and unseen.

This is the challenge. Too often people offer good advice or wise counsel from the space of the ego, the *You*. This form of input has a particular vibration. Though helpful in some ordinary aspects of how to live in the world, it doesn't offer the resonance of soul truth that opens space and creates soulful pathways forward in energetic awakening. When it is couched as coming from the soul and for the one receiving this guidance not tested for a sense of rightness, it can be coercive and deeply confusing, building up more ego constructs instead of supporting in the release. It's not that this form of guidance is bad, it simply isn't in full resonance with the space of the soul. You want to always feel for rightness within, to what is offered from another about your soulful growth. There may be pieces you can take or ways that you feel accuracy below the spoken word. Or, you may sense ego speaking and simply say thank you and move along.

Dismantling Guidance of the Soul

You will know the voice of the soul because it breaks apart. The soul seeks a return to essence, encouraging form to fall away so that more of life is lived from the vast expanse of no-thing. No longer are the unseen worlds simply tricks to access or information pathways for guidance about how to live life. Rather, these worlds rise to meet you and become your primary source of identity. They become the place in which you now live. In this way, the world that we have known fades away, and this new world, a world of wonder and magic, becomes your new home.

Soulful guidance from the depths often has a dismantling quality. Guidance from the soul leads to greater awakening in one's life. The path of the soul is not the path of the world and the outcome of soulful guidance looks different. Divine guidance has a quality of pointing you more deeply inward to your truth, even when the messages are difficult and not welcome.

Divine guidance often points toward dismantling, not building up more of you. This is an essential piece—divine guidance that comes from the soul often points toward breaking apart what has been of ego up to now, thus being in service to the soul having more space to live within you. The soul isn't interested in all of the well-formed aspects of your life like your job, living circumstances, financial well-being, or even how family is constelled. It's not that those pieces aren't important to the fabric of existence, they certainly are. The difference is that your *You* has an idea of how it all needs to be ordered and arranged for you to have a "good" life and this is what is being undone. You remain in the world in a common way, doing the tasks of ordinary life. The difference is that you don't tell your soul how that will look. Your soul, through divine guidance, guides you.

When the Israelites were wandering in the wilderness they demanded a sign from God, something to pacify the bitterness of their aches and fears. The heavens rained bread upon them and they were filled, at least for the time being. Along with the manna delivered daily, they received words of guidance. "Gather what you need. Do not leave any behind. Gather enough so you can rest on the seventh day." They did not listen. For the mind knows what is best. Take more than we need. Leave some behind. Do not listen. The manna rotted and molded and so did the people. The bitterness resumed as did the demands for another sign from heaven. The guidance from the soul will only speak into what is good for the collective soul. The voice of guidance that rises from the *You* is primarily focused on the *You*.

From within the stillness, there is no efforting or analysis about what is wanted. It is a position of allowing where you are more a channel than the originator of what arises. This is crucial both in receiving your own guidance and in receiving guidance from others. We want to feel for vibrational rightness, allowing the messages from the soul to stay and those of the ego to float away.

Receiving Guidance From Your Soul

Divine guidance rises from the stillness within where you now have space to hear beyond the chatter of the mind. It is from within stillness that you are out of the way enough (though there is still more release required in awakening) for something wiser and more expansive than you to come forward. Divine guidance only flows through a hollowed out instrument that rests within stillness and releases the need to know or form a thought.

At this point your guidance can take many forms that feel concrete, where you are able to directly engage with a knowing that emerges from the unseen spaces. You are beginning to step into a stream of guidance that always flows, and stillness becomes the access point from which to hear the living guidance that is available to us.

We know when divine guidance is rising because of its quality. Have you ever experienced offering an idea at a staff meeting that felt like it came from somewhere else? And maybe there was a particular kind of silence that resulted? The *You* often takes credit for these moments, but they are really your soul speaking. They tend to feel like a hit that courses through you in a moment in which the mind is offline.

During some seasons we have worked with guides, angels, and ancestors. At others our work was in the subtle/energetic realms. Guidance can come through picture, etheric sight, wordless knowing, audible messages, symbol, dream, natural visitations and many, many more ways. The form is not what matters, but rather the space that it comes from.

Engaging the Unseen

We refer to these spaces as the mystical (divine beings), natural (nature), and subtle (energetic) worlds, though over time these categories will become less distinct and the need to name what you are receiving less necessary. This categorization is merely a way of describing the guidance that is rising and allowing some handle holds for your learning and experiencing.

These realms open within and around us, connecting us with the oneness that holds us all. Our ability to listen from within stillness—the no-thing—is the starting place for allowing something unseen and unknown to rise. So, for now, know that those are the spaces that you are accessing as you listen into the guidance that rises within you. Making them distinct can help you orient to what and how you are hearing as you expand your awareness.

What you are listening to is what emerges from stillness—the no-thing—that allows guidance to rise. In this space you have no expectations and your *You* has no say in what is delivered. You are yielded to allowing what is there to rise and to receive with openness what is delivered. As you practice releasing into the stillness, more space is created for something to speak from this space. You will not know beforehand what might rise and you can't manage what shows up from that space. You release completely and simply allow the rising to well within you.

All awakening phenomena are pointing you back to the soul within. Whether the songbird you notice that accompanies you on a walk or a spirit guide that speaks in your ear or a surge of energy that courses through your body, all are orienting you to pay attention to how the guidance of the soul is with you.

Jesus invites us into the guidance of the soul that is all around us. He gathers his followers and points them toward what is living and breathing all around them right before their eyes. They can't miss it. Do not worry about your life. Pause and look. Do you see that bird, this field, even you? This unworried existence is not an illusion. It is real. Do not worry about what you will eat or what you will wear. Enter into the field with me. Actually stand in it, not with the mind, but within it. Do not stay a distant viewer of the birds of the air or the grass of the field as though it is only for them but not for you. That worry-free existence is real. "So, it is for you," he says. The care that is for the grass of the field (which is here today and gone tomorrow) is also for you. It is for all. It is when your mind holds you separate from the natural world, rather than in sacred reciprocity with, that you scoff and say that what is for one is not for the other. It is only in your own illusion of separation that you will say this is true. The soul speaks what truth the mind will not see.

During this season, you will allow these communications to be recognized and engaged. This often takes some readying to receive. First, you notice something present that is slightly outside of your grasp and awareness. It can be a flicker of light, a press on the back, a movement of energy within, the arrival of a snake resting quietly in the sun just before you. What you may have simply moved through or ignored creates a pause and in that emerging moment space is made.

At this point the urge is often to figure out or name what the "something" is. We want to place a description on what is rising. This often leads to whatever is arising going flat and then going away. Instead, you soften into the quiet place of the soul, feeling from within the experience in this moment. The mind goes offline as you ease down and back allowing everything to stay as it is. There is no need for anything more to show itself.

Then, as you abide within this softening stillness, you expand out around your body into the unseen spaces around you. You feel from within this space as if your skin, your sense abilities, are extended out 360 degrees around you and every pore is open to receive whatever is there. You accept the simplest sense—a twinge at your back, a cool breeze across your face, the sense of light and movement before your eyes, the snake raising its head ever so slightly to look directly in your eyes.

Again, instead of reaching out to what this might mean, you soften inward again, deepening even more and simply allowing. You are becoming one with the unseen space around you in a deeper interconnection that will deepen more and more as you become more diffuse and allow the space to open more and more.

Each one of us has a primary sense or two that will initially serve as an access point for rising guidance. They typically fall within our known senses to include seeing (either in front of you or in etheric space), hearing, knowing, feeling, sensing. These sense awarenesses open as you still more and more. They often begin as whispers, fragments, quick flashes, quick knowings, bodily senses. If you latch on to what rises, it goes away. If you follow what is rising from within your experiencing, like a guide who is leading you somewhere, your sense awareness will continue to increase and become more sure and other sense abilities will begin to tune in and come online to add richness to what is emerging.

The movement over and over and over again is release. Anything you try to understand or grasp narrows and goes away. What you learn to follow from within experiencing opens more and more and becomes a guide to you, leading you deeper into the landscape of the unseen.

Subtle Realm Rising

The subtle realm is the unseen spaces of energy around you that can be both experienced and followed for guidance. The energetic awakening journey is most essentially about learning to track these energies from within your experiencing in everything. The more you listen into this space and allow it to open, the more you will feel the energetic movements of awakening.

Energy has long been heralded for its healing qualities, even for the most staunch of skeptics. Jeffrey D. Rediger is an instructor at Harvard Medical School and studies what some call "miracles" and what the medical community calls "anecdotes" or "flukes." He researches those diagnosed with a verified terminal illness who experienced it move into remission. Jeffrey promotes a counter ideology in his work to the "miracle" or "fluke" explanation. We only know the tip of the iceberg of mental and spiritual laws. What we do know is that perception changes experience, even to the point of changing our physical bodies. In the subjects he studies, it is through the absence of fear and the presence of the soul (or as he calls it the Kingdom of Heaven) that the physical body reflects our inner energetic reality. More specifically, Dr. Rediger points toward physics, how the universe behaves and the motion of space and time, as the frontier for modern science and the key for understanding how energy works.

As the world rises to meet you, you will have opportunities to directly engage these energies and to learn how to follow them. You may see energy as light around and within a person, in landscapes, in flashes. You may hear the movement of energy, sense energy, feel energy, know energy. Whatever your access point, the movement of energy is communicating, asking us to notice, follow, be within.

The vibration of energy will teach you to track balance and flow, noticing where energy is moving and where it is not. As beings made of light and vibration, energy is the essence of what makes us what we are. Subtle awareness allows you to enter this essence space and learn its communication. Over time, energy will be as real as the objects in the room where you are now sitting. It has qualities, textures, movements, senses, connections. You can feel it within your body as an extended felt sense and you can see, feel, hear, know it in your surroundings. It will become the instant communicator of rightness and dis-ease. The knowing of what wants to change and what wants to stay as it is. It will show you where lack of movement is creating tension in your body and it will show you how this is mirrored in the larger world. The subtle realm will guide you into entering spaces where you can track non-local processes, meaning knowing things when you aren't actually there, and ways where healing happens by the energetic vibration that you hold.

The subtle realm is the space of creation and action in the world for it is the substance of it all. To open and connect to the subtle realm is to gain access to ways of knowing that will open you beyond what your mind can now conceive.

You can begin to sense subtle energy by trying to feel it, see it, sense it. Often people will use the energy between their palms to feel the texture of energy as you move your palms close together and then further apart. You orient to the space between the form, your hands, and notice any qualities about it that are noticeable, even if just a little. Or, you can have someone stand against a white wall and soften your eyes to see the halo, the aura, that rests around the human body. This can be a color, a shadow, or simply a sense that you practice with. You are training your sensibilities to perceive what is unseen and it is important to remember that what you see or sense is not an endpoint. It is a passageway into something more.

Over time you may feel the larger constellation of energies within a space—a room that you enter, the hairs raising on your arms as you walk down the street, or the sense of rightness or of something off in a meeting. You may notice that you attend to the qualities of the constellation of energies—whether they are dense or heavy, if there is something drawing your attention. You may shake someone's hand and get an immediate sense of who they are even before speaking. All of these movements are tracking and noticing energy and how it is providing guidance and reflection for you. You may enter subtle space and notice that you are uncertain about where you end and the larger space begins.

As we work with subtle energy we become increasingly aware of the light and vibration that is us and is in everything. When we sit in a meeting and review a spreadsheet, there is an energy to the conversation that we feel ourselves being within and no longer separate from. All of these movements are entering the guided landscape of the subtle world that will continue to open more and more.

Mystical Realm Rising

What we call the mystical realm is often known as guides, teachers, ancestors, angels from the other side. As you awaken, you begin to experience thin space or etheric space in which these presences become more palpable and alive to us. Whether you know them by a voice that you cannot identify or see them as clear as the light of day, they are here for your spiritual companionship and awakening journey.

Dr. Eben Alexander was a neurosurgeon who understood well what happens to the brain when we are near death. He awoke one morning with an extreme headache that landed him in the E.R. and a diagnosis of a rare bacterial meningitis. He spent seven days in a coma and when the medical personnel were determining whether or not to discontinue treatment, his eyes opened. Upon recovery, he described an experience of higher consciousness and a dimension that he could not verify scientifically, as the neurons in his cortex were completely inactive during the coma.

What he recounts is that for his journey in dimensional space and time a young woman accompanied him. She had golden brown long tresses, a lovely face and plain clothing. It was her radiance, a vivid aliveness, that captured him. She would look at him with complete and pure love that was not romance or friendship. It was universal. She spoke three truths to him. "You are loved and cherished, dearly, forever. You have nothing to fear. There is nothing you can do wrong." As he recounts, he felt an instant understanding, as though someone had handed him the rules for the game he had been playing, but not getting the hang of. These are the unseen companions of the mystical world and their purpose is to show us our truth.

Many brilliant teachers have created a system of identifying and understanding the unique purpose of these phenomena. While specific guidance for your life from these beings may rise, the overarching and consistent message is to show you the truth of what you are, your essence and your vibration. These worlds are not always gentle or docile. In crossroad moments, there can be a visceral movement, even a push, to take the next step in our awakening path. Whether we literally feel the unseen hands of an ancestor on our back or the eagle that circles over us time and time again, or the burning sensation in our hands that will not cease, their guidance is consistent and direct. Do not go back to sleep. Stay awake.

Like all phenomena, when you enter into the sacred reciprocity with the beings that companion us, you are open to the truths they bear. These beings are in their fullness and they are granting you a window into a fullness that you are growing into. They mirror to you what you cannot always see in the physical world. The world will reflect an image of illusion to you, but the awakened world is the mystical world. The mystical world reflects perfection and union. It is seeing this reflection of wholeness that casts a glimpse into what we are returning to, and the palpable awareness of being surrounded and supported at all times in the community you need to open your path.

You are companioned at all times. You are never alone. In any given moment, like right now, you can use the movement of noticing, softening into, and resting in stillness to begin to connect you with these unseen companions. The mind will tell you there is nothing there and want you to dismiss any rising awareness that is getting your attention. You simply notice, soften inward again, release the assessment of the mind, and you rest again in stillness without expectation or need for anything to happen.

As you feel this movement over and over, you will begin to allow an opening to appear. This is an access point for guidance to make its way through the density of mindsets and ego and begin to land in your experiencing. You may see, know, sense, hear, taste, smell something. A simple mantra of *I am willing* will allow the guidance more space to come through until the channel is open and you more freely receive the communication from the ever present support gathered around you.

When we enter the mystical world, we will encounter beings of light that are here for our highest and greatest good. You will know what you are encountering from your spiritual sensibilities that are unique and perfect for you. Trust your intuitive guidance. Often our mind will discount what we are feeling or wish to juxtapose it against our lived experience. Remember that these beings are appearing to you in a way that is to assist you on your journey.

When encountering an ancestor you might begin to feel a sense of a paternal or maternal connection moving and shifting. This may be paired with a visceral sense of recognition. You may notice a familiar smell or a voice in your ear that recounts a family ideology. You may begin to feel a clearing movement as a generational construct releases or opens. We often know ancestors (whether we have actually met them or not) by feeling a connection of familiarity—as if they have always been there and that there is a bond that we can track and orient to.

When we encounter a spirit guide, we may not have the same familiar aspect. There can be a feeling of longevity as though they have been with us for all of our lived experience, but it is a different quality from family. Spirit guides often carry a palpable light and vibration that captures our awareness and serves as a catalyst for our awakening. When you begin to expand awareness, you may feel a sense of concentrated light behind you. Whether you see the being or not, these are often spirit guides that are here to companion us. You may feel a vibration in the space in between where you and the spirit guide connect. This is where we begin to connect to the guidance they communicate to us. It may not come in words but in pictures or visions. Again, they are here to encourage us into our highest expression. There are endless types of spirit guides that many intuitives explain in great detail. To keep it simple, there are guides who protect us, teach us, coach us and assist us in our lived existence, and they often change as we grow and develop. As we continue to expand spiritually, there is often a changing of the guard to support us in our awakening.

Angels often appear especially in times of change and

transformation. There are countless angelic beings and four main archangels—Gabriel, Michael, Raphael, and Uriel. Knowing the specifics of these beings is less critical than tracking their essence and when they appear. We know angels by their size and strength of light and vibration. It is unmistakable. Angelic beings often break through our awareness and call us to follow their energy. We are compelled to notice and respond. Many people have experiences of angelic beings in moments of great distress or trauma as their force has a way of breaking through the physical plane and providing a sense of rescue, protection, love, direction or guidance that we cannot turn away from. They can always be called upon for support to assist, protect, and heal.

Natural World Rising

The natural world is most verifiable to the mind and you will likely find this connection one of the first that opens in your spiritual sensibilities. Like the mystical world, there are many systems that comprehensively define meanings for phenomena. The beauty of the natural world is the endless facets of expression that exist. In a raindrop that crawls down a window pane or the rapid beating of the hummingbird's wings that ring in your ears or the rhythmic rocking of the ebbing tides, we are bathed in the gift of the natural world. It is calling us back into a natural, balanced order within. To live in freedom and synchronicity once again instead of the separation that our modern world has created.

Eutierra is a newly coined term to describe what has been called that oceanic feeling in spirituality. It is the marked feeling of oneness as the boundaries between self and nature fall away. It is being connected intimately with all of life most visible in the natural world. Even spending a few minutes outside has been shown to change how you feel and a few hours can reset your endocrine system.

Alexander von Humboldt was a naturalist and explorer from Prussia who lived from 1769-1859. As a child, he collected and labeled different plants earning the nickname "little apothecary." Into his adulthood, he could be found studying in the morning and searching for plants in the afternoon. He became one of the foremost contributors to the earth sciences for his writing, research, and travels. It is his relationship with the natural world that is his greatest legacy.

He writes of eutierra as the sacred relationship present with the natural world. This relationship is not one of receiving nature's benefits. Rather he points to the face of nature that draws us into the soul within or that oceanic feeling. He pens, "Nature can be so soothing to the tormented mind, the blue sky, the glittering surface of lake water, the green foliage of trees may be your solace. In such company it is even possible to forget the reality of one's personal existence."

Simply being in the natural world for a period of time will open you to its secret wisdom that is perfect for your own understanding. Rather than staying with the phenomena as containing only one message, the guidance from the natural world will meet you where you are in the moment you are in. Once again, it is in its fullest expression and it will reflect to you the fullness of you as well.

You may begin by simply being in nature more often— taking walks, sitting by a tree, watching the bird feeder outside of your kitchen window. By placing yourself within nature you allow its awakened perfection to begin to naturally infuse you. The benefits of simply resting within the arms of the natural world cannot be overstated. You will experience healing and release as her rhythms right you and support your return to a balanced energy flow.

Nature is also a passageway to deeper connection with the unseen. Everything is connected and by allowing something to capture your awareness—the feather on the ground, the glistening in the leaves, the pulse from the large oak tree as you rest your hand upon her. Each of these moments are opportunities to listen more intently to the rising guidance from within the connection.

Again, many people develop systems about what all of the symbology means. This can be a beautiful reflection of the communication of the natural world, but it doesn't take the place of deepening into the connection. We don't want the meaning of a bird to end with a description. We want that knowing to open us into something more that we can then follow energetically and allow to open within us and open us to receiving from the larger, unseen world.

As we abide in nature, she becomes a teacher to us if we follow the movements of noticing, softening, and deepening into. We learn that the alive communication of the natural world are ever present and infinitely wise, ushering us back home into the truth of what we are.

You can begin to hear these messages as you engage with the natural world. You may notice nature reaching out to you in some way or you may notice a proclivity for an aspect of nature. You may resonate with a tree, water, birds or the very earth you walk on. Noticing will begin to allow messaging through what you are attending to. You can begin to be more aware of how one aspect of nature begins appearing to you. Even now you may notice ways that the natural world is speaking to you. Feathers may appear along your way—on your car door, stuck to your sweater, dancing in the wind as you walk. Many traditions will define what a feather means and this is a helpful starting point. If you feel the energy of the feather and hold it in your hand and connect with it, it has a specific message for you. Like listening to a spirit guide, it is by noticing the space in-between you and the feather and being in that space that the communication and guidance will emerge.

Over time, you will begin connecting more directly with aspects of nature and entering in communion into the spaces in-between. You may sit with a tree and feel a connection that is beyond words and your own personal experiencing. You and the tree, or the river, or the entire expanse, will feel a relational connection that opens more and more.

Over and over again you are living into engaging into the essence and vibration of the natural world for how you are within it as part of an ongoing communication and guidance for you and with you. From this place, you can sit under a tree and connect with the treeness that it is communicating not just to you but to everything because it just is. These markers of awareness, a feather that appears, a hawk that circles, the wind that blows a window open, are more distinct moments to break through our slumber and call us to awaken.

Guidance

You will have your own unique way of receiving guidance that will develop over time. For some it will be auditory and you will hear or simply know something that you know you don't know. For others you will see or feel guidance in images or symbols, or through pictures or subtle energy. For some guidance somes through a channel and for others it is more like waters you swim in that become more clear and knowable. Here is an example of a place where the mind will likely try to take hold of what is arising and make judgments about or attempt to manage the guidance that is coming through. You may find yourself making assessments of capacity or judging your ability against others. Or, you may begin allowing guidance to rise and then questioning its validity as the mind wonders and manages.

We receive guidance in a variety of ways and this has changed over time as we continue to open and live more fully from within Divine Union. We learn to follow rather than lead and we open into energetic, vibrational, and dimensional spaces where the healing becomes less and less effortful and more about positioning and allowing.

Guidance comes through each of us in a myriad of ways and the quieting of our *You* allows us to yield into how and when the flow of the divine will move through. All expectations must be released and allowed to transform for there is no right way for divine guidance to come through and it always points toward something rather than answering with authority a question. Moreover, as you learn to listen for the rightness of emergent guidance it feels more like a pointing toward than an answering of something. Over time, you can work with others in the space where guidance is received from, each person feeling in their own way toward the unfolding truth that is guiding us all.

As you live from within your depths within the stillness of no-thing allowing guidance to rise, it will show you how it moves through you teaching you how to relax more fully into allowing. You do not guide this process and it lives outside of time and expectation. You are in a space that is leading and opening you to what has always been there. It does not matter whether you see, know, sense, feel or hear. What is of the essence is that your sensibilities continue to open and communicate with you with ease and a sense of release. For what is guaranteed is that when you begin to attach and hold on to one way of knowing, awakening will shift this sensibility. It is relocating you back into the soul's intuition. The ego wants to make a spiritual gift into something to master. What has been given to you is to be offered without attachment. From this positioning, more will open.

What would it be like for you to be in this silent space as much as you are in the talking, thinking, functioning location within? You may realize how little you may say. When we begin to listen into the guidance that is within and around us, we notice how full our meetings, our dinner tables, our car rides, and our recreational time is as we listen to our inner chatter instead of the voice of wisdom that lies within and around us. Your guidance will land solidly in your circumstances rather than dance around the edges of ego. The car ride with your son can be filled with listening silence for what wants to be spoken rather than what should be. The mundane tasks at work are all listening moments in which you feel for rightness of how they can be done with a lighter step, easier pace, and rest within. The workout that is one more thing to fit in becomes a moment of awareness of what is good for you. It may be that the 30 minutes of sweat shifts from ruminating about how much you need to get done to an appreciation of your body's capacity. It does not need to be profound. Running on the treadmill does not need to be a super moment of connection with a spirit guide. If you are aware, though, how your soul wishes to speak will rise.

Over time you notice that you are dwelling in the depths of stillness. This is your home. There is no need to move out of this place in order to figure out the world. It is from here that you will meet and see the world differently. This is of the essence. You will not see, hear, sense or know in the same way for the soul has its own sensibilities that do not map on to your *You*. There is a place of wonder in this location as, for a time, you may experience more nothing than something. By allowing the nothing to become your new home, a fresh something will rise in its place.

Energetic Experiencing

This is the world that is ready to show you its truth. Things are not as they seem. Illusion is not present in these depths. What is clear will be pure in its communication and there is transparency in how the world will appear. This is not built on surety. It is clarity. This world is sparkly with its newness and as clear as a new day. You do not experience this world via constructs. It only rises in seeing what has always been there, only now for the first time.

1. **Center:** As you center and come home, take additional time to allow your *You* to quiet. As we step into the world that is rising to meet us, there is a small release that must occur. Like traveling through the eye of a needle, there is a pinch point, threshold, a narrowed passageway. There is no way to see with the eyes of the ego or know with the gut of the *You*. It is only in their suspension that we enter a new world. You may wish to breathe a mantra or prayer of yieldedness to assist you in dropping within. Let it be basic—a few words or a breath.
2. **Rest:** Like slipping into a deep sleep, settle into the depths you now know to be the soul. There is a patience here for you must know how to be in this space until you can no longer differentiate between you and the soul. In other words, it is abiding within union. You may find time slowing or becoming non-existent. Or, the edges of what you perceive as you and other becoming one.

There is a full and complete release in settling in. You are entering liminal or etheric space. You will find that you cannot orient too much. All of this is indicative of being in between rather than in form. It is in this space in between that the world rises.

3. **Open:** Begin to notice what rises. Expand awareness gently beyond the edge of space as you perceive it. You will notice that you will sense movement out, up, down, etc… beyond the edges. You may feel as though you connect into or feel into a something. You may see, hear, know, feel this something. It may be heat, vibration, energy, light, coolness, tingling. There are not enough words to capture this experiencing. Trust your own sensibilities.

These are phenomena of awakening that are pointing you home. You may begin to notice guidance emerging in various forms—vision, word, sense, emotion. Stay within the guidance that is rising from the connection into spiritual phenomena. Guidance is a passageway to carry you deeper into the soul. Stay within. Let it guide you.

The world that rises to meet you is a reflection of your soul. This is essential to understand. Spiritual phenomena are not the end. They are a beginning. They are passageways of opening, expansion, and growth. As you receive guidance, know that they are always present to point you back home and to go deeper and deeper into the awakened world within. There is much joy and elation as the spiritual sensibilities open. Relish in this delight. Enjoy the sacredness of communion with the unseen world. Listen carefully. Even the guidance which is most specific and concrete in your lived experience is emerging to assist you in your return, maybe even in guiding you into moments of detachment and release so that your soul may continually open. These are your companions on the journey and their only goal is to bring you back home. What good news! For so often you have felt alone in this world. Finally, you know the fullness that has been with you and that is ushering you each step of the way.

7

FALLING INTO UNDOING

Zaccheus was a wealthy tax collector in the town of Jericho and he wanted a chance to see this man Jesus for himself. Zaccheus was short and he knew that if he stayed among the crowd he would be barred from view and so he climbed a large Sycamore tree. As Jesus passed below Zaccheus he called to him by name. He told him to come down and he declared that he would stay in his house this day. Can you imagine? Being called by name by this infamous man. Zaccheus immediately climbed down from the tree and simultaneously fell into his own undoing for his next utterance was to give away half of his possessions and if he had mistreated anyone to give fourfold what was owned.

The crowd was in an uproar for Jesus had chosen to stay in the house of this sinner. Zaccheus had heard the message and responded, for that is where undoing comes from. It is our next step into coming home to the truth of what we are.

When you realized the two worlds—the surface waters of circumstance and the deep waters of the soul— and began navigating between them, allowing divine guidance to rise, you still maintained control of your life. You had the capacity to engage a conversation about where you were and how you wanted life to be and the ability to decide for your *You* was still within your grasp. Remember, to live with a foot in both worlds allowing soulful awareness to inform the ordinary circumstances of your day is a gift to you and to the world. You can live a happy, spirit infused life staying planted within your circumstances and dipping into spirit to refresh and infuse and allowing divine guidance to lead you without full relinquishment of control.

This is the moment, however, where a choice must be made and control relinquished to continue on. The reason this is a threshold is that from here there is no turning back. No matter where you find yourself now, you want to pause and listen from within stillness to the rightness for you. There will be times along the path where you will wonder what is happening and you may question whether you wish to continue on. And that is why it is a point of decision. You must give a "yes" for the journey to continue. The yes is given by your soul and it is your agreement to participate from here. This path is not forced upon you and you can decide (in some ways) whether you continue.

THRESHOLD CROSSING

The first step is your agreement to cross over. You not only relax your grip on life, you now release completely. At this point you give control to your soul. This moment of choice may be made consciously, but often it is a deeper, quieter yes given from within. Simply knowing this is a marker along the way can help as you enter the season of undoing. It will not last forever. It is only a season.

Undoing is a process that will continue for the rest of your life as you continuously yield to the unfolding of life. You are developing a reciprocal relationship with the unseen spaces around you abiding completely within the depths of the soul while staying connected to the larger world around you. You fully embody being in the world, but not of the world.

In order to rest fully within this new space within there seems to be one season of tremendous undoing that continues the process of dismantling and reorienting. It often picks up momentum during this time as many pieces of your outer world re-order.

You may enter this threshold with an idea that much is changing and you have compartmentalized what you wish to pack for the crossing and what you are okay leaving behind. This undoing is comprehensive in that it is teaching you to live without ego constructs and with an unequivocal "yes." Leave your bags behind. What you carry with you is deep within and what is born of the soul will stay with you no matter what.

Led By Your Soul

It can feel like the difference between cleaning your house each week and doing a deep, Spring cleaning. The awakening path has worked to clean your house of pieces of *You* that no longer serve. You've tidied and sorted, dusted and polished many of the surfaces of your life.

The great undoing is Spring cleaning time. It's as if your soul takes the duster out of your hand and goes through every drawer and closet, removes anything no longer needed from the surfaces of life and boxes them up to be removed from your house. It can often feel like you are simply a bystander watching the trophy being boxed up and the clothes sorted without much power to stop it. You might find yourself utter, "Wait, I need that" or "Don't take that away. That was expensive" as your soul simply continues the packing and removal of anything no longer needed.

There are pieces of your life that you know need to go. You don't need the things that really aren't serving you. It's the pieces of life that look good to you and the world, the ones you have worked so hard to achieve, the ones that have an emotional connection that create the most protest from you. You may begin to wonder what all of this is about—questioning the rationality of this season—resentful of the changes.

You will likely even experience a loss of connection to the sweetness of the rising guidance that brought you into this season. The delight of connecting with the subtle, natural, and mystical realms will shift during this time and it too may feel that it is falling away—being boxed up and carted out of your life.

It can sound ominous and not very welcome to engage this process. That is why so many decide to keep their life as it is and to dip into the deeper realm of spirit on a schedule while keeping hold of the steering wheel of life. To have access to your soul, but to maintain life as you know it can look very good from the outside. You need not fear. There is nothing that will fall apart that is not ready for release. Undoing does not barge into where there is not already micromovements of falling away.

This is where many spiritual seekers have bypassed or stopped the journey of awakening. The undoing process brings up every unresolved issue and faces you with pieces of your life that you may have avoided until now. The tendency might be to blame someone or something or to attempt to be super-spiritual for the things before you can feel very earthy, mundane, and unwelcome.

Yes, bypassing this process—avoiding, ignoring, or trying to float above it—may all feel like viable strategies for survival. Unfortunately, this stops the process of awakening from continuing, with the added cost that because you've said yes to this process, bypassing results in a dose of pain from the resistance.

Wandering in the Wilderness

The movement in this season is a continual stilling, allowing and yielding. You will likely find it difficult to locate yourself anywhere, for you can no longer identify places of security for your placement in the world has fallen away. At times it can feel like there is no ground to stand on and that your place in the world is shifting day to day. Do not fear. This is changing your position so that you can relate to everyone and everything from a different perspective.

You may feel profoundly lost during this period of disorientation— there will be much that you do not know, and you'll likely be able to speak more into what you don't know than what you do. If you tend to label who and what you are this aspect of the undoing can be deeply challenging. Whether you lose the actual titles and names that you once held or if they simply lose meaning, it will change you. Again, this movement is so you know what you are beyond identifying markers of what you have done or accomplished.

It harkens to wandering in the wilderness— being lost in the desert. You will likely become like a wanderer without a home—even if you still have your literal home base. You may experience a lack of fit just about everywhere—in your job, at home, with relationships, with the very routines that you've used for so many years. This is not an abstract reflection. All of this is lived and experienced deeply. As things begin to crumble and fall apart you will feel the barrenness of desert landscapes surrounding.

John of the Cross, venerated as Saint John of the Cross, was a Spanish Catholic priest, mystic, and a Carmelite friar who sought reform and paid the price. He faced increasing opposition, misunderstanding, persecution, imprisonment. In his imprisonment, John uttered poetry from the depths of his being, depicting the dark night of the soul and a time of wilderness. His enduring words are a reminder of what falls away and falls together in this time of undoing.

> *"Upon a darkened night the flame of love was burning in my breast*
>
> *And by a lantern bright I fled my house while all in quiet rest.*
>
> *Shrouded by the night and by the secret stair I quickly fled.*
>
> *The veil concealed my eyes while all within lay quiet as the dead."*

Falling Away of Identity

This is likely the most radical shift during the Undoing. Your orientation to any identity is gone—the loosening of all cords tied to your ego identity—the names you've called yourself, the things you have done, what you feel you need for safety, the people, places, and things that surround you. What may surprise you is how many cords there are and how impacted you are by their release. No longer can you call yourself or your life by any of the names you once did and it can feel like you are standing in a vacant expanse—naked and exposed. Even an experience of pain or sadness shifts during this falling away as you reorient more directly within the soul. This process is more internal than the dismantling of the structures and pieces of your life that might involve jobs changing and relationships altering.

The process of falling away is deeply disorienting partly because our surrounding world encourages the building up and solidification of a self in numerous overt and subtle ways. The idea of not having an identity doesn't even make sense and as you consider this in your own life you may wonder what this means. The situational circumstances will look different, but the path of identity release is essential. And, often, that which is deemed "spiritual" or "religious" or "of God" must be reworked for their true nature to emerge. Practices and routines that were of our *You* fall away in order for the essence of the soul to come forward. Nothing is outside of the scope of undoing.

This is what makes the great undoing markedly different. It sweeps away all that we hold. It gives you nothing to hold onto that you can identify with as your own, as what you are. All of the things that defined us, including our suffering, are all undone so that they are no longer a source of identification.

So, let it go. It is not part of where you find your primary location in life. Let go of the jobs, let go of the homes, let go of the cars, let go of the friendships, the relationships that are part of our definition of self, for they do not exist anyway. The soul exists beyond these categorizations, the soul is where love dwells. And where the definition of love emerges that is beyond any one thing to love or to be attached to and this is where your soul abides.

Where Did My Mind Go?

In this process, you may feel like you've lost your mind—literally. It is as if all of the aspects of living in the day-to-day world evaporate and you are left in open space. You may experience forgetting appointments, losing details you would have never before have forgotten. You may find yourself in an open landscape wandering more and acting less. This unfolding process is the relaxing of the mind and is a key waymaker—a deepening into that you felt pieces of as you began your awakening journey, but now feel all encompassing. Do not be afraid. This process is making space so that you are not as full of thoughts that spin and go nowhere.

In this state, you may find routine questions insurmountable. The simple query of "paper or plastic" or "coffee or tea" requires a movement back into the *You*, the surface waters, that you've left further behind. For, from within this emerging new awareness your orientation is shifting from the *You* to your soul essence where you can no longer name or claim what you once could. From here the lapses in thought become greater to the point in which remembering simple tasks requires recall and a sense or connecting back into what has been lost.

We have plenty of stories of checks not cashed and ordinary opportunities to order from a menu becoming insurmountable obstacles to overcome. Simple tasks that would take no more than a quick internal check for desire or what feels right became places of open space where nothing rises. You may be caught unawares by this as you are unable to reference your preferences from your *You*. The curious piece is that it isn't as distressing as you might imagine, just strange, for the timeless space of all that surrounds becomes the place where you now walk.

You may imagine the frustration of those around you where your once appreciated competence becomes languid meanderings in the fields around your house or workplace. You are inhabiting more of the timeless space of unity and the practical details of the day are completely out of awareness. What feels like an open expanse to you can become the frustration held by everyone around you as you ponder how to answer the question about whether you want a refill on your water. Really?

At times this absence will feel like freedom from the constraints that once bound you and at other times you will feel absent, lost, slightly panicked, and removed. We found this season to be almost comical and we appreciated the orientation to the awakening journey during its unfolding. Spouses commented on tasks that went undone and on the aimless space that we seemed to inhabit. It was as if we were in a different realm and life lost the clock that once ticked us into action.

People may need to step in and do things for you—keep your schedules, respond to emails, take over your accounting. The routine tasks that were second nature become hurdles to overcome specifically because they don't feel relevant in the same way and whatever energy the ego used to manage those tasks is no longer online. This, too, is part of the falling away and the reorientation to the soul within the great undoing. The gift that surrounds you is a web of support and care that is present during this time.

The mind does return so have heart, but it will never rule you the way it once did. Rather than coming from without and orchestrating the movements of your life, the mind will rise within as rightness that is felt and from there, next steps are acted upon. The timeless space that now surrounds is no longer ruled by the clock or pressed upon through the *You*. You learn that the inner manager of the mind is either absent or comes forward when needed to do the grocery shopping and to attend to the schedule. No longer does your *You* dictate how and what gets done in life. For, life is now lived from the soul.

Companioning

You are not alone. You are companioned by the unseen spaces, and those who are on the awakening path provide presence for you to continue. To gather with those who walk the awakening path can be a support along the way. To know that you are not alone is often enough to continue on the journey.

Your relationship to the larger unseen spaces will also

shift and open. You will feel divine support in the spaces in between as you open more fully to life's leading. It may not look like it did before the Undoing. Often the unseen realms become less formed and discrete meaning that they cannot be accessed and seen in the same way. They are present nonetheless and will deepen you into their living landscape more and more as you let undoing move away all constructions and impediments.

Through all of this, you will learn that you are not alone and you never were. When you experience this truth, everything shifts. Actions born of fear slowly dissipate and you no longer need to act from the anxious place that is afraid. You learn to lean on unseen support and find that there is a blanket of comfort at all times.

Do Not Be Afraid

Do not be afraid in the great undoing—it has its time and its place—it has its purpose. The goal of this undoing is to reorient everything, to undo what no longer fits, and to place you in your new home, the soul. You will find yourself in a new terrain filled with lightness as what once was dear and also a burden no longer holds the weight and centrality that it once did. A sense of peace and tranquility emerges as you stand on new familiar ground, experiencing your new location that transcends the circumstances of your life experience. Freedom comes from undoing for the very things that we used to hold as sacred, and untouchable in our life— be it where we live, our family life, our work life, what we held as meaningful— is changed.

We have watched many students and clients traverse this landscape to discover that what fell away during undoing was not necessary. What was ready to release fell away naturally and was not missed. There may be some pain and an inevitable resisting at first. Once release was allowed the shifts happened on their own and created freedom. That is the mystery and beauty of letting go completely. And this is the paradox: while everything is falling away, a greater peace emerges beyond any ability to understand how it holds us. That is the gift that comes in this falling away of the great undoing.

Energetic Experiencing

Believe that you need nothing that is falling away. The soul needs nothing. What is consistent in this process is that from nothing there is a rising movement that emerges. So, it is with undoing. While incredibly painful, there is a hidden grace in each attachment that untangles and makes space for a new way of being to emerge. Do not bypass the pain or tears, the kicking and screaming that may accompany this movement. You may protest and rail against this movement of awakening and yet there is a difference.

Can you feel that there is something larger within the falling away? That it is not a depression or sadness or grief or loss that has a hollow ring to it? No, there is something larger that is present that is ineffable. It is only through knowing that we can access this persistent message that what is falling apart is somehow leading you into a new place that you could not access on your own. It is the step off the ledge. It is the crossing over. From this undoing, nothing is the same. And you would not want it to be. The newness of life is no longer for temporary visits. It is permanent and so your life is also being reordered around this new permanent home. You are awakening and you cannot go back to sleep. Your exterior life will not allow it to be so. What is changing is also keeping you awake.

1. **Center:** You will find that you are consistently

living from center now. Occasionally you may find a slipping out of alignment, but the movement to come back in presses on you almost immediately. This is a gift in times of undoing. No longer do circumstances in your life bring the same modes of comfort. Staying in center is your focus for it is what sustains you. Take a moment to appreciate this fixed point within.

2. **Falling:** As you expand awareness, you may begin to palpably feel the cracking, dissolving, splitting, shifting movement in your life. Allow the grief to rise for what you have held dear is reordering your soul. It must change shape to connect in this new way. Fall into the movement of reordering. There is an energetic movement to falling away and it wants to carry you into reorientation. You cannot step around this movement of falling into the undoing. It is what will place you back on firm ground once again. It is not comfortable or easy. When you feel wobbly, ask for help. The unseen realms are your companions.

3. **Standing:** Follow the movement of disintegration. When you feel as though the loss or grief is too much, stay in the present moment. Your mind will want to make sense of what is happening. This undoing is not furthered by understanding, but by present moment awareness. As you are present in time you will find a moment of reorientation. You will need to wait for it. Maybe one minute. Maybe one year. There are micromovements that are slowly placing the ground of being underneath your feet. This is your why. The undoing is leading

you into being. This is unshakable peace. No fear. Living in stillness.

Your *You* will not like undoing. Who does? You will want to step out of this process over and over again. Yet there is already a pervasive stillness within you now. This is what is causing the changes. It is this stillness that will be your guide and your respite. Return to it over and over again for one second, one minute, or one year. It will not fail you and it is rewriting your life to usher in an awareness that is without story. It is connecting you with everything that was and is and will come. You are alive and you are here. You are no longer observing your life. You are in it.

8

ENTERING A NEW WORLD

Hildegard of Bingen was a visionary, a mystic, an herbalist, and a composer that was born around 1098. She had many mystical visions beginning at the age of three that continued throughout her life. Hildegard spoke and wrote about humans as living sparks of light using her literary and musical gifts. She described this light as 'the reflection of the living Light' and she was instructed by God to write down all that she sees.

From within this light-filled landscape Hildegard witnessed all of humanity from universal wholeness. She began to radically and prophetically describe men and women as part of a greater harmony with the whole of creation. She began to communicate this vision as she wrote over 300 letters to those who wrote to her, spreading this vision of harmony, unity and equality and left a legacy of 'visionary theology' for future generations to receive.

You have now entered a space where the world that you know has fallen away and another world has opened. These two worlds are no longer separate—they are one and the same. It is not the world that has changed, it is your relationship to the world that has shifted. Your orientation is now in your true home, the place of the soul, and from this position the way that you see and engage the world is forever changed.

You may notice more and more that the space that you are in is alive in unexpected ways. We call this space *Your Awakened Landscape*. Over time you will feel this space as a location that you abide in—a place full of connection and sacred reciprocity with both the seen and unseen worlds. It is simply a landscape of energetic movement that you will learn to be within and track. As your journey continues from here you will begin living within your awakened landscape in everything. It will become as real as the chair you are sitting in and as obvious as the room that surrounds you. Your awakening is beyond your own story and you now inhabit a timeless, dimensional space.

Awakening Landscapes

An awakened landscape is a space you position yourself within in order for something larger to open around you. You had access to this space when the world began to rise to meet you and you connected with the unseen through the mystical, subtle, and natural realms. They are still one and the same. There is no difference between them. The difference is how you can dimensionally position yourself within the larger unseen surround to open more fully. It is the difference between being within something and simply having access to it. What once you could only look in or step briefly into for guidance is now accessible to you completely.

Positioning in Dimensional Space

The undoing allowed for this new positioning. Now, not only are you positioned in center within your soul, you now have access to a position within a larger dimensional space.

You might want to imagine this dimensional space as a large sphere that surrounds you. To place yourself in position is to be poised in the very center on a pivot point within the large sphere. This central positioning is active, not static, as you steady and ride the movement in this space. Your position within center is what either allows the dimensional space to open or stay flat.

You can imagine geometric grid-like patterns that run throughout this large sphere where everything and everyone is connected. You can visualize them as facets of a diamond where each surface catches the light differently and reflects. Or, you can see them as fractals or geometric shapes that connect through intersecting lines to infinity. It really doesn't matter how you describe it. The point is to be within it and that is what your new ability to position in center allows.

There are aspects within this space that are part of how energy comes through and what allows manifestation to either come forth or fall flat, meaning whether it goes somewhere in the world and creates or just stops. That process is one that tracks manifestation energies in your own life and in the larger world. For now, simply knowing the movements for how to position will give you access to this unseen space for you to begin exploring in and learning from.

Your awakened landscape is yours, but it is also connected to the space of divine union—the space where we connect with everything in its wholeness—the grid of energy within dimensional space. It is most essentially an inner positioning that connects you more fully to the unseen space of energy and to the larger connection to realms where guidance comes through. The difference from simply receiving guidance for insight and information as you may have done previously is that you are now within this space in everything. No longer do you simply listen in to the guidance that comes through the ever present stream. Now you are within the space yourself and you become a connection point from within this wiser landscape and your life becomes a conduit of divine energy to the world.

Over time, your awakened landscape will teach you and communicate with you in your particular symbology—a heart/wisdom language that you develop and listen from within everything. It will have all of the facets you might imagine—sight, sound, sense, picture, feeling, intuition—and more than your mind can conceive. It will develop over time and your landscape will become a communicator and teacher to you as you listen more deeply from this space.

Entering with Others into Awakening

The beautiful piece is that you can enter another person's landscape and listen within from your vantage point or you can extend this to working with a group where all participants connect from within their awakened space in a vast interconnection of gathering as each person becomes a point of awakened light in the whole. Over time, you will be able to hold the larger world from this space. It can feel far out and yet very grounded in experience for this space is infinite and specific all at once. You can know this literally, as if seeing with your eyes in this space, but it requires a positioning within to access and maintain.

We will say more as we go, but for now feel yourself in your centers within and from there begin to expand outward into the space around you. See yourself within a sphere—like resting at the central pivot point within a three (or four or five) dimensional beach ball, right in the center—for this is where you will now rest within your awakened landscape.

Dimensional Positioning: The 5 R's

In order to access this space you begin to open and track an inner process following energy where you position within your center—not just in your Sacred Heart Center and Sacred Wisdom Centers within—but dimensionally in the larger unseen space that surrounds you this space opens.

All of the movement in the spiral of awakening led to a central space of center, the stillness of no-thing. You can likely feel right now that clear sense of when you are in your center. When you are in your center, you are home.

To place yourself in dimensional center—in the center of that beach ball around you— and to begin to feel the energetic movement in everything, you open into a moving, flowing center— a placement— that does not have an end or an arrival point. Rather, it is a bodied sense of what center is that is calibrating and adjusting in relationship to the larger space that is holding you at all times. *Dimensional Center* becomes a home base where a living conversation between you and all that is has an unending opening. Positioning is crucial. And so there is a process that will help you more fully access and abide in this space. Learning to position in this placement is central to opening into living a guided life where you become the receiver and transmitter of a higher vibrational guidance that is made manifest in the world.

There are 5 R's that support the movement into dimensional center. Each of these offer an energetic process that you can track from within your *Awakened Landscape*. They will open you more fully from within the larger dimensional space that surrounds you and help you to begin to track your own process from within the space. You will also begin to develop your own sense-abilities and enhance your way of sensing beyond what is seen only with the eyes. Through this process you are learning to develop your own awakened landscape and from here you are in collaboration with other souls who have awakened and are in the space of divine union. Remember, you are learning to follow energy, not to attain something. They are simply movements you follow to carry you into center.

Receptivity

There is an opening into— a readying within— that enlivens your placement within dimensional center. One way to describe it is to say that you place yourself in center and then open outward 360 degrees into the larger unseen space. There is a volitional movement of positioning yourself in this way followed by an alertness to the larger space. You allow every pore within you to open and accept information beyond your seeing eyes and knowing mind.

Receptivity is your sense awareness. You open into it like opening the pores of your skin to allow them to sense and receive. If you feel around you now with this open awareness, sensing beyond your skin, you begin to orient and allow a richer sense awareness to emerge. You are following an energetic movement in this process—one that teaches you to track it over time. It is where your sense-abilities will develop and then fall away for they are simply a portal or starting place from which to then allow even more information to flow. The stance of receptivity is the readiness to receive beyond the mind. You are open to an energetic movement that will be unnamable. Practicing your positioning with receptivity will train you to sense this space more fully from within your experiencing.

Receptivity is often referred to as "open to experience" where individuals are intellectually curious, creative, and imaginative. Openness to our experience allows more information to flow into our visual system allowing us to see what others may block out. Researchers have found that people that are *open* can feel complex emotional states because seemingly incompatible feelings simultaneously break through into their consciousness. In this way, openness to experience invites us to literally see the world differently.

In the classic research study, "Invisible Gorilla" test, researchers showed participants a film clip of several people passing a basketball back and forth and asked them to count the number of passes between players wearing white and to ignore the players wearing black. During the film, someone in a gorilla costume wanders in among the players and begins beating their chest. Amazingly, most participants in this study reported that they did not see anything unusual or surprising during the clip. We tend to see only what we wish or are focused on.

Openness and receptivity encourages us to see what is often blocked out. By learning to allow a state of receptive awareness to guide us we open to the world in a new way. Receptivity changes how we see our own life and our perspective with the world. It expands our awareness to see the world as it truly is.

Release

Like the movement you have already practiced in *stilling, allowing, and yielding, release* drops the mind away and all of the aspects of your *You*—especially the ones that critique whether you are doing it right or applaud you for your giftedness in accessing dimensional space. Too often the mind gets in the way of the process of energetic movement opening you into more of what is. Just when you think you've arrived you must once again release whatever has been attained to sink more fully into this wise, always opening landscape. You let go of what you have collected and come with open hands filled with nothing. There is a famous Zen story about release that is told and retold and published and republished as it fully embodies release.

Two traveling monks reached a town where there was a young woman waiting to step out of her sedan chair. The rains had made deep puddles and she could not step across without spoiling her silken robes. She stood there, looking very cross and impatient. She was scolding her attendants. They had nowhere to place the packages they held for her, so they couldn't help her across the puddle.

The younger monk noticed the woman, said nothing, and walked by. The older monk quickly picked her up and put her on his back, transported her across the water, and put her down on the other side. She didn't thank the older monk, she just shoved him out of the way and departed.

As they continued on their way, the young monk was brooding and preoccupied. After several hours, unable to hold his silence, he spoke out. "That woman back there was very selfish and rude, but you picked her up on your back and carried her! Then she didn't even thank you!

"I set the woman down hours ago," the older monk replied. "Why are you still carrying her?"

Learning to release what you know is continual. The movement of release will become as familiar to you as your breath as you feel the catch of settling or the thinking around success. Like letting your breath flow out and down, you ride the release yet again sinking more deeply into dimensional center remaining receptive and open for what is present and yet unseen to simply be as it is. A something. A nothing. It doesn't matter. You are within this space completely devoid of expectation or need.

Rightness

You will feel for rightness as you begin to track energy—learning to notice where it lands, when it is ready, how it is moving. You will have your own unique way of reading for rightness, but it will have a tangible quality to it. Rightness has a feel that most often lands in the body in a certain way that communicates.

Take a moment to feel when something isn't quite right. It's like a picture hung crooked on a wall or a yes to a generous invitation that somehow doesn't feel right even though your mind doesn't know why. As you feel this, you are tracking energy. When it is off, even slightly, you stay unsettled in some distinct way. When it lands, or connects, or moves smoothly (however you want to feel this energetic movement), there is a sense of relief—what we call rightness—that moves and opens you into what is next.

Feeling for rightness is the place where you begin to notice energy and it will teach you how it moves. This form of energy tracking is not linear, but multidimensional. As your awareness from within this space increases, the vast interconnections of all that is expands more and more.

Steve Jobs, the visionary co-founder of Apple, in his 2005 Stanford speech, credited knowing inner rightness as having a significant impact on his work. "You have to trust in something," he said. "Your gut, destiny, life, karma, whatever." He added, "This approach has never let me down, and it has made all the difference in my life."

Jobs had a specific strategy for connecting in with his inner wisdom: walking barefoot. He was well known for engaging brainstorming meetings while walking around barefoot in order to feel more clearly how his ideas were landing and moving within him. This is the kind of rightness that is known from head to toe.

Rightness will become the wave that you ride from within dimensional center as you feel probabilities and learn to be poised in emerging potentials that are not yet rising as you wait at this pivot point. When rightness lands energy moves and you learn to follow from within the emerging experience. You are in the ride rather than looking at, understanding it or simply experiencing it for the moment.

Receiving Guidance

Here is where divine guidance comes from. Guidance that emanates from this space is limitless. Where before you were enchanted by the threads of guidance that came through (and we, too, know how exciting this can be). Now, you are within the place that all guidance arises from and you learn that positioning is everything. When you place yourself within dimensional center and learn to fully abide here, you live from within guidance where it comes forth in everything.

The great Buddhist teacher Thich Nhat Hahn was very close with his mother. Upon her death, he describes a time of extended grief and mourning. One morning, he experienced a shift in the weight of his grief from this point of guidance and connection with her. He wrote the following in his journal reprinted in The Buddhist Review Tricycle (2021):

> *"The day my mother died I wrote in my journal, "A serious misfortune of my life has arrived." I suffered for more than one year after the passing away of my mother. But one night, in the highlands of Vietnam, I was sleeping in the hut in my hermitage. I dreamed of my mother. I saw myself sitting with*

her, and we were having a wonderful talk. She looked young and beautiful, her hair flowing down. It was so pleasant to sit there and talk to her as if she had never died. When I woke up it was about two in the morning, and I felt very strongly that I had never lost my mother. The impression that my mother was still with me was very clear. I understood then that the idea of having lost my mother was just an idea. It was obvious in that moment that my mother is always alive in me.

I opened the door and went outside. The entire hillside was bathed in moonlight. It was a hill covered with tea plants, and my hut was set behind the temple halfway up. Walking slowly in the moonlight through the rows of tea plants, I noticed my mother was still with me. She was the moonlight caressing me as she had done so often, very tender, very sweet... wonderful! Each time my feet touched the earth I knew my mother was there with me. I knew this body was not mine but a living continuation of my mother and my father and my grandparents and great-grandparents. Of all my ancestors. Those feet that I saw as "my" feet were actually "our" feet. Together my mother and I were leaving footprints in the damp soil.

From that moment on, the idea that I had lost my mother no longer existed. All I had to do was look at the palm of my hand, feel the breeze on my face or the earth under my feet to remember that my mother is always with me, available at any time."

You become a vibrational connecting point for guidance— a channel that allows the voice of spirit to speak apart from ego— your *You*, into another's landscape and into the world. Guidance becomes something that you are within in everything. You may choose to simply listen in for your own life, without any intention of helping others in a direct way. This awakened position requires a commitment for you to become a channel to the world. No matter where you are at —in a job, bedridden, in prison, or sitting at home folding laundry—your position matters in and to the world. By holding dimensional center from within your awakened landscape, you become a portal for a higher vibrational energy to move forward in the world making change beyond the mind. To hold center from within this awakened space is the change that the world most needs.

Reciprocity

An alive space. It is how it is meant to be. When you live from within your truth allowing your present receptivity access to the unseen spaces around you, an opening and connection occurs with the tangible world and the energetic spaces beyond our sight. You will learn to live in sacred reciprocity with everything in the ongoing communication between all that is.

In the 2019 TED's *"How to Be a Better Human"* series, Joann Davila, a professor of psychology and the director of clinical training at Stony Brook University identifies the 3 core skills needed for a healthy romantic relationship. As she notes, "We may know what a healthy relationship looks like, but most people have no idea how to get one — and no one teaches us how to do so." According to Davila and her colleagues, there are three core skills behind romantic competence: insight, mutuality and emotion regulation. Specifically, it is mutuality that demonstrates how we live in reciprocal relationships not only with our romantic partners but also with all of life.

Davila's research shows that mutuality's core tenant is about knowing that both parties have needs and that both sets of needs matter. Specifically, she studied 18-to-25-year-olds in relationships and found "the more romantically competent men and women felt more secure in relationships. They also reported making better decisions ... They were also better at seeking and providing support to their partners, so they were more willing to ask for what they need and use what their partners give them. And they were better at providing helpful support when needed."

This is how we listen. This is how we learn to live in harmony with our surroundings. This, awakened living, opens up an ongoing sacred conversation that will not end. We become the breath that breathes us as a channel and witness to the oneness that surrounds us all. You are within the larger connection of everything, receiving and returning, the beauty of light from which we are all made.

Living Life Awake

Awakened living is how you walk toward true center allowing life to lead you through each moment in connected flow. By living each moment, consciously, fully aware of not the reality that you see, but the reality that is unseen that is emerging. You learn to appreciate what is still foggy and murky, for from within your awakened landscape you are tracking the energy, allowing the 5 R's to guide you in the moment, and you know that your position is the power that will change the world. You are within the experiencing, no longer separate or walking apart. You now walk in alignment and your life becomes a living meditation.

To live into this dimensional center is to know that there is only love in this world, and what you see as shadows are really your own limitations to see what is of love moving beneath its surface. We often want to make our life situation be something other than love, but if you are willing to listen to it at its core, you continually hear the invitation of the

Divine to dwell in love, abide in love, to be one with the love that is always around you and within you.

Imagine how our world will shift as more and more people awaken on this planet and begin living from their truth—the position of the soul. Feel into the implication of not seeing others as separate from you where you build dividers and walls to keep out what is unwanted. Imagine how living in the world, but not of the world will alter the landscape of ordinary moments within families and in corporations that can't help but notice the interconnection of everything and how their decisions impact the whole. Notice what your light being feels like as a contribution to this world, living from a higher vibration that enhances and enlivens rather than depleting and depressing. And then feel your ability to connect dimensionally from within divine union where you have access to a living conversation of creation with every piece of our precious planet and beyond.

Energetic Experiencing

You are living in a world of union— in the landscape you are within at all times. No longer do you need to go locate yourself in a sacred space in order to find connection. It is with you always. From this position, the spaces around you will also come to light—or actually you will see them as they are. The awakening light sees light present in everything. You will find your world shifting in response. It is not as though anything has changed, per say, rather the space you hold awakens and so you will see the awakened state in all. It is by living into this state that is present everywhere that the awakened landscape broadens and becomes all encompassing. This is not an end point for you. It is a resting place though. For what greater delight than to begin to see awakening in everything and everywhere. You are connecting into the essence and vibration instead of the ego form. From this all things are possible and probable.

1. **Center:** You know now what it is to live from center. Your *You* will still rise from time to time, but there is now an understanding within. There is no going back. Moments of ego flicker here and there, but there is a renewed steadiness within that rises from the centered position. Allow your awareness to expand and feel center from within your awakened landscape.
2. **Follow the R's:** Bring awareness to this spaciousness. You may notice that even reflection comes from a different orientation now. It is not mental. Gently open and soften into a receptive state. Allow what rises to emerge and release any attachment or connection to it. Feel for rightness within as you hold what is rising in your awareness. Receive the guidance that is emerging. Allow it to rest within you. Feel the sacred reciprocity that you are living this guidance and that there is a mutuality present.
3. **Completion:** Continue to follow the movement of guidance in your experience. As always, let it guide you without effort or force. It is in the movement of reciprocity that it will continue to open and expand you. There truly is nothing for you to do.

You will live in constant flow with these 5 R's as you awaken into a guided life. No longer can an errand to the grocery store be unconscious. Each moment of each day, each interaction, is guidance. You need not look for it. It will present itself to you with abundant clarity. It does not mean life will be ordered and neat. However, no longer will the messy moments be charged in the same way. All experience is welcome. Nothing is siphoned out. This is the movement of living in union as you embody the endless cycles of *receptivity, release, rightness, receiving guidance* and *reciprocity*. Soon they will not even be in your awareness. You will live them as you sleep and as you are awake. They are in everything for this is how the soul lives.

9

LIVING A GUIDED LIFE

Mechthild of Magdeburg was a Christian Medieval mystic. She was born into a noble family and she experienced her first vision of the spirit at the age of 12. She left her home in 1230 renouncing all of her worldly possessions and embarked on a mystical path.

Mechthild was a leader in a 'before their time' early women's movement. As a member of the Beguines, a Roman Catholic laic order, she lived and prayed in an enclave of women who expressed holiness outside of the norms of Catholic monastic life. Lifelong celibacy was not required. Informal vows of ministering to the sick and poor bound the community together without the many trappings of the monastic order. It was an inherently mystical community often labeled as heretical free spirits. With this free spirit, Mechthild sang and wrote of love—divine love. Her descriptions of love grow from moments of mystical ecstasy like an unrequited lover aching and yearning for God. Her hallmark work is "The Flowing Light of the Godhead" in which she describes passionate dialogues between God and the Soul in the manner of a courtly lord wooing a queen in court.

She does not solely focus on divine union as the apex. Instead, the conversation is primary. It is the movement, the living dialogue, that leads toward union. It is the lovesick ache that opens greater expanses of love and the burning desire within that is the call to draw closer into union. Her words clearly capture these dynamic conversations in the back and forth— the push and pull— the yearning and longing. *"Lord now am I a naked soul and Thou a God most Glorious! Our two-fold intercourse is Love Eternal which can never die."* Her words capture the guided life, a sacred dialogue that unfolds in the now. Born of free spirit and outside of the confines of form, this is the conversation of union and oneness. There is no end to the flow of conversation that rises from the energy of divine love. It is the guided life.

Life is an ongoing conversation. There is never a moment where the energy of the universe stops infusing you. There is never a moment where you are out of reach of this ongoing flow. Being positioned within dimensional center is the key to access this larger space—the space of emergent, energetic conversation—spirit incarnate in the world.

A New Paradigm

This is the new paradigm. What was once named and described is now felt and lived from. You use your sense awareness to track within experience and this becomes your guide in everything. Your positioning opens up the space allowing you to follow unfolding experience in each emerging moment. What was once of the mind—in thought, form, construction, description—is released completely. There are no more handle holds of the mind. The mental constructs of form have fallen away in order for energy to take center stage and to begin to live through you, through us.

Practically speaking, no longer is what you see with your eyes the real world. This is a radical shift from the mattered world we have lived within thus far. Until this point, we have described life by what we have seen or known. A chair is a chair. What is right is what is right. Some things are wanted, others not. This way of orienting to life was the very fabric of our daily existence.

It is often in a moment that our world shifts and we see something anew. Valerie Cox penned the following story to characterize the shift of awareness available to us.

A woman was waiting at the airport one night,
  With several long hours before her flight.
  She hunted for a book in the airport shop,
  Bought a bag of cookies and found a place to drop.
  She was engrossed in her book, but happened to see,
  That the man beside her, as bold as could be,
  Grabbed a cookie or two from the bag between,
  Which she tried to ignore to avoid a scene
  She read, munched cookies, and watched the clock,
  As the gustly "cookie thief" diminished her stock
  She was getting more irritated as the minutes ticked by,
  Thinking, "If I wasn't so nice, I'd blacken his eye!"
  With each cookie she took, he took one too.
  When only one was left, she wondered what he'd do.
  with a smile on his face and a nervous laugh,
  He took the last cookie and broke it in half.
  He offered her half, and he ate the other.
  She snatched it from him and thought, "Oh brother,
  This guy has some nerve, and he's also so rude,
  Why, he didn't even show any gratitude!"
  She had never known when she had been so galled,
  And sighed with relief when her flight was called.
  She gathered her belongings and headed for the gate,
  Refusing to look at the "thieving ingrate".
  She boarded the plane and sank in her seat,
  Then sought her book, which was almost complete.
  As she reached in her baggage, she gasped with surprise.

There were her bag of cookies in front of her eyes!
"If mine are here," she moaned with despair.
"Then the others were his and he tried to share!"
Too late to apologize, she realized with grief,
That she was the rude one, the ingrate, the thief!!!!

This is why it is a paradigm shift. We are being reoriented by this larger space that is guiding us, shifting our awareness and perspective to movement rather than to form. The former structures of our world are breaking apart just as you have been. Matter must fall away so that the world can return to a tuned in reciprocity, a living, unfolding conversation with the larger world around us. Where we once sought clarity and surety we now swim within the waters of unknowing, allowing each unfolding step to guide us, as we follow the emergent movement of energy in everything.

To live is to awaken—to be here in the world completely from within divine union, the interconnection of us all—and to allow all of life to be lived from this space. There is no separation, anywhere. Life is about awakening to this, moment by moment, hour by hour, day by day. Our return home is a return to this place within where we release everything, hold nothing. Our life becomes the breath that breathes us allowing the vibration space to reverberate throughout the world. The simplest act generated from this place is the needed movement to energetically awaken the world around you.

This is a new paradigm. It is a new way of engaging the process of awakening—an energetic process where you collaborate with the unseen spaces around. It is energetic in nature meaning it is alive and must be followed in everything in order for it to continue. The tuning within to these larger energetic movements becomes the rhythm that lives each one of us in everything.

The New World: Essence and Vibration in Action

Those who hold this dimensional presence become sparks in the world. You allow essence energy to flow through you while you vibrationally connect and allow this energy to flow into the world. To connect with all that is of this earth and what is of the heavens (the cosmic realms) simultaneously as well as being within what was and is yet to be within time and space is awakened living. You open to the vast interconnection where your roots go deeper into the dirt of this earth as your crown expands higher and higher opening to a vast network of interconnection.

Margery Williams in her classic tale, *The Velveteen Rabbit*, describes becoming real, becoming awakened, and never going back to sleep again. This is where we feel the interconnection with all of life bound by the fabric of love.

> *"What is REAL?"* asked the Rabbit one day, when they were lying side by side near the nursery fender, before Nana came to tidy the room. *"Does it mean having things that buzz inside you and a stick-out handle?"*
>
> *"Real isn't how you are made,"* said the Skin Horse. *"It's a thing that happens to you. When a child loves you for a long, long time, not just to play with, but REALLY loves you, then you become Real."*
>
> *"Does it hurt?"* asked the Rabbit.
>
> *"Sometimes,"* said the Skin Horse, for he was always truthful. *"When you are Real you don't mind being hurt."*
>
> *"Does it happen all at once, like being wound up,"* he asked, *"or bit by bit?"*
>
> *"It doesn't happen all at once,"* said the Skin Horse. *"You*

become. It takes a long time. That's why it doesn't happen often to people who break easily, or have sharp edges, or who have to be carefully kept.

"Generally, by the time you are Real, most of your hair has been loved off, and your eyes drop out and you get loose in the joints and very shabby. But these things don't matter at all, because once you are Real you can't be ugly, except to people who don't understand."

But once you are Real you can't become unreal again. It lasts for always."

Those who are awake are called to stay fully engaged in the common aspects of life in order to affect consciousness through grounded and active participation in the world rather than by separating from the world. This new paradigm is the feminine way where you remain where you are (in terms of ordinary life) while orienting in the Soul. This is illumination. By living into the Soul, everything becomes holy (even dirty socks) in that it expands from within you and illuminates all that is around you.

Living Dimensional Connection

This lived awareness becomes your life landscape in the ordinary that you inhabit and becomes connected in profound ways to all that has been and is yet to come as well as what is of this earth and that which is beyond—you become unbound, diffuse, and as a consequence you travel (or exist) dimensionally—within everything through space and time.

You loosen all constructs attached to this life, no longer fearing any circumstance, including death or annihilation.

For when you awaken you are within your dimensional home that is not just the heart center, but a gateway or portal within the infinite. You will find yourself journeying without ever leaving where you might locate yourself as existing, allowing a form of action to move through you into the world.

In this process your light body, the essence of you, becomes more diffuse, deepening your humanity and expanding your reach. You become more grounded while being more divine. Your presence in the world is more fully expressed because you are not as attached to the world. There is less of you and more of spirit shining through. You have created space and more of your light flows out into the world.

You learn to follow energy in everything developing an emergent awareness of how energy is moving in your life and in the larger world. These movements are trackable and you can develop your energetic awareness where the stories that have bound you fall away and an ability to follow energetic pathways rises. You are within this landscape.

Even as you read these words you may sense that to identify what you call *You* is now ineffable and ungraspable. You are no longer the definable *You* that you once were. Feel the expansion of light particles that emanate from your source body and how you begin blending like a drop of distinct color added to clear water moving within and through and into. You are more diffuse and with fewer borderlines. As a consequence you are within the world and yet not of the world.

Energetic Awakened Action

It is from here that awakened living flows into the world. You are now a divine channel allowing flow to move within and through you touching the world as you go. You are becoming a conduit of awakened action as your life is guided through this ongoing energetic movement. The larger expanse that holds you orchestrates beyond what your mind could ever conceive and the delight that arrives is how divine encounters appear, next steps unfold, and how change manifests in the people and world around you—naturally and easily.

This is awakened action. Action no longer comes from the constructions and good intentions of your limited ego mind where you end up creating what you never intended and having to deal with the impediments of resistance. It is no longer bound by an ethic of transaction. This new paradigm alters the need for outcomes and allows an abiding no matter the circumstances.

Hear this story from this space. Kenneth Collins was a police officer at the Metropolitan Police Department in Washington D.C. in 1963. He was tasked with the job of protecting Martin Luther King on the day he delivered his historic "I Have a Dream" speech. In every photo, Collins is in the background standing close to King. As Collins describes, King approached the microphone and the two exchanged a brief glance. "I could tell by his eyes the type of person he was, and when he talked, I was convinced." Collins, now 78, struggles to put this energy into words. "I can't explain it—you had to be there." This is the presence that makes us say, like Collins, "I've never heard anybody talk like that."

This is the presence filled, action moving, alive state of being that Jesus embodies in the story of Mary and Martha. Martha is moving, working, keeping up, efforting and making the world work. Mary is entranced. "I've never heard anybody talk like that." It is all about the living energy that speaks beyond the words that are delivered. This dimensional connection into what is beyond is present in each moment that Mary steps into by sitting at Jesus's feet.

No longer is she oriented to her own self in conversation with Jesus. There is a larger, living connection that beckons her. You can feel her yieldedness, willingness, receptivity in being guided and led by the energetic presence Jesus embodies.

As you hold presence in the soul, your light influences the fabric of all that is (what it is already within) for there is no separation. It is no longer up to you to figure out rightness or make things happen in your circumstances. You work in vibrational, energetic spaces and when something manifests in form—movement, steps taken, situations engaged—processes move along almost without effort. You are living union with the divine.

All movement that comes from this source expresses itself in fullness in the world without the need for an assessment about whether it is right or good. It will always carry a transformative quality because it is awakened and will spark awakening in the world. From this, everything can change even while perceiving that "nothing" is happening, nothing is changing, or no action is occurring. It is when we think that nothing is happening that awakened action is emerging. If you think, you are not acting in flow.

The beautiful outcome of this way of living is that you will now walk in this world as if you are a part of everything and this means that your creations—your actions and intentions—work not just for you, but for the whole, especially the actions of divine union.

This is true transformation for it changes everything—especially what you might perceive or judge as inaction. There is no longer a duality in your living—no good or bad, in or out, and even no right or wrong. To live is simply to be the channel and wherever you go and whomever you touch is sparked to awaken for your presence. You are now the instrument, the hollow channel of divine flow living life from within each moment in simplicity and with lightness.

And, from within this place of allowing you become an authentic change agent in the world because of your positioning. When you live awake, you naturally awaken others as you go.

Awakening the World

This is what will move our Earth into a new place of consciousness. As more and more energetically awakened beings in this world live from their true home it will bring the world with them into a higher vibrational state.

For, in order for this earth to survive, we must live into an awakening that is not built on trying or seeking an outcome. We can no longer attempt to effort or work with our good ideas and just causes. Those methods are born of the *You* and are limited and finite at best and are often coercive, creating more of what we don't want at worst. It is time to allow source to live through us in everything, everyday from within the higher vibration of divine union where, by staying present to our awakening and aligning our life with this consciousness, we influence the very fabric of existence.

This is a positioning of strength. To hold stillness from within dimensional center in the midst of an unconscious world is to bring forward awakening. It is a natural impulse to want to make the world a better place. For eons we have done this very work and heaped good intentions upon good intentions upon good intentions. It is not a passive positioning to hold stillness and presence. It is one of power in that it is holding awareness until the impulse quiets and true action emerges. This requires full awareness and a willingness to go beyond what life is presenting to us into the dimensional, liminal space where we are not just reacting to this moment in time but providing presence across all of time and space.

As you learn to follow these energetic movements, not

from the mind but within what is rising, you open into a space where true sacred reciprocity is possible. You are within living energy and you follow it in everything.

The awakening that waits for us is our positioning within this consciousness where we allow our life to be an instrument, where life flows through us as we align ourselves more fully with divine union, getting out of the way and allowing, becoming the conduits of healing for a world that is groaning and aching. In that way, it is the epitome of it not being about the *You*, but about how we all stand in the collective. How we are one and in oneness with what is around us at all times. There is no separation. By elevating beyond ourselves, we elevate this world.

For now, the journey has just begun for it will carry you both now and forevermore. Your saying yes opened before you the expanse of purpose that your heart seeks. You noticed the sparking, separated and began to live from your soul, opened to the mystery that surrounds us at all times, allowed the parts of your life that no longer fit to be undone, and from here you walk within the world from a different place. It is this positioning that the world has been waiting.

Know deep within you that you now live within the vibrational matrix that will sustain you and support you in absolutely every moment of your existence. You have made the most consequential step in your human walk upon this earth—it is why you are here. To awaken is to come home to the truth of what you are. And as you go, your presence will touch an aching world longing for their own return.

Walk gently upon the earth allowing your identity to thin more and more and watch how people begin to wake up, just for your presencing, as you go. And, as in all things, the journey will continue for awakening is never complete. Overtime, you will learn to track energetic processes more and more and be within them completely as they guide you deeper and expand you more broadly into the vast interconnection that holds us all.

Live forward from here within the unity that holds us all, for you are now home, positioned within, just where you were always meant to be. You are connected within the vast network of time and space living from this truth as you go about your life within the simple and ordinary. Do not doubt your contribution or analyze your impact. To live from within your soul is to live awakening. When you live from here you awaken others and this is the change that will save us all.

EPILOGUE

Common Awakening was created to support people on the awakening journey— it was created for you. For all of us, the awakening journey is guided by something larger than the mind as we learn to follow the energetic movements from within experiencing rather than from the constructions of the mind. As we've journeyed with many people who are awakening, it takes about a year to live fully from within center—center within and then within dimensional center— and then from there to learn to track and work with emergent energetic processes from within the experience.

We invite you to join us in our online programming and at our intensives to find support wherever you are on the journey. The lull to go back to sleep is strong and touchpoints in our daily life help to support us in staying awake. And, there is more to learn, so please join us in learning how to continue to open into and work with the movement of Energetic Awakening at *commonawakening.com*.

As you learn to live awake in everything you become a spark to the larger world around you. This is how awakening will begin to move our planet and return us all to the essence truth of what we are, lived forward into all of life through the vibration of action in our world.

We look forward to the journey!

ABOUT THE AUTHORS

We haven't known each other for very long, but our guided path brought us within each other's orbit—unknowingly 17 years ago—and again just over three years ago, in order for Common Awakening and this book to come forth. Something larger that holds us all, organized and orchestrated right timing for this writing to be made manifest. Our schedules opened and words flowed through, allowing a fresh perspective on awakening to come forth. This new orientation is common in it's perspective, meaning it is for everyone.

We are rather ordinary people. The focus of our days are on raising our families, living within the meaningful work that calls us while doing mounds of laundry and dishes. At times the fabric of our life is a loosely woven tapestry that at any moment might begin to unravel and yet within all of this everydayness we feel deeply called to share this message of awakening. We invite you to join us as we allow awakening to spark within everyone—in all of the common aspects of everyday life, within the muddle and mess— in order for us to live more soulfully as we walk embodied in the world but do so positioned within our true home, our soul.

Annie's Awakening

My earliest memory is of my mother's face looking down at me lovingly and noticing the glow around her. In fact, the whole world glowed—a sort of luminous, dewy existence that came from seeing clearly, knowing everything and needing nothing. My world was not separate. The clouds danced with me. The wind spoke of secrets. My pet sheep's eyes reflected the world to me. I spoke to ancestors who lingered by my bed at night. The rainbows around everyone's form were as clear as their faces. I knew union before I knew of separation. We all do. That is what makes this story unique and yet the same.

As is the story of humanity, my world began to change as I grew and formed. The rich landscape dulled a bit as my mind conformed and the reflection I found from the adulted faces in my landscape upheld a rigid truth of what was real and what was not. Slowly, the union I knew hid within me, masked by a put on logic that I desperately worked to uphold. Occasionally, the curtain would drop and I could see and know again of this unified space before the mind quickly gathered itself up again and the curtain closed.

I pursued classic Christian mystical texts in my adolescence. For once, I felt as though it was a language that I had longed to share with a trusted friend in huddled conversations. Childhood was a struggle at times—feeling a lack of fit rather than the hand in glove match. Like many who may read this, I had an old soul in a youthful body and the mismatch felt too much to bear some days. When the mystics came along, I felt a language within me returning that I couldn't find replicated around me. Meister Eckhart, Henri Nouwen, Thomas Merton, Teresa of Avila, John of the Cross and others became secret friends that I felt oddly connected to across the ethers.

I followed the path of high school, college and graduate school and subsequently spent years in ministry and non-profit landscapes. I also created the landscape of my home and family life. Life was ticking along and I was following the prescribed path. I knew enough about awakening and mystical experience to hang with the best of them. I prided myself on being one of those spiritual people—even an awakened one. For mentally I was awakened and I knew all about divine union, states of consciousness, mystical experience and spiritual formation but knowing about was different than actually falling into it.

One day, six red-tailed hawks roosted in a tree in our suburban yard and stayed for 10 days. My mind failed me for how to explain this phenomena. Each day I went outside and spoke to them. All I could say was "I'm listening" and a deep "yes" began to rise within, from that luminous space I had forgotten so long ago. One day they left and the dissolving of me rapidly began.

For all I knew about the masculine tale of ego loss and subjectivation, I wasn't prepared for the anguish that tore through me and the immense grief that companioned me for years. The curtain fell and did not draw its place again. Liminal space opened and became the place from where I lived. So often I wanted to leave and go somewhere, anywhere, as though leaving would somehow coax my ego to come back out of hiding and resume its location within. I began to live beyond thought and the world opened up its beautiful face to meet me.

I continued to walk in the liminal space around me as part of my awakening and it invited me to deepen into what is, even as much was rapidly falling apart. So I deepened into raising my children, loving my partner, folding my laundry and driving my minivan. I often wished for a more dynamic awakening. However, as I held a state of consciousness and presence in my life, everything changed. Undoing rapidly opened and I found myself knowing that I wasn't going back. Rather, I was returning.

It was after years of waiting for a holy moment of arrival, that something in me laid down and said "yes" to the awakening being as it was. There was no glorious Teresa of Avila moment of being pierced through the heart like I anticipated. There was unspeakable joy and freedom. There was a centered infallible peace that could not be moved, no matter what circumstantial undoing moved through me.

This is where I sit today with no sense of anything other than now. I am awakening beyond my mind and the world looks as glorious, luminous, and wondrous as my childhood. I am no longer leading my life. The divine world guides me. The liminal space that opened is my home and is not separate from the physical one I inhabit. The layered space of souls around me, the song of a robin on my path, the clear eyes of my child, the awareness of energy coursing through my being and the ground of peace beneath my feet are all mirrors of union. My mind is quiet, my heart is open, my soul is alive. All is well. All is well.

Annmarie's Undoing

My story is one of return—a return home to something I've always known. For as far back as I can remember I have been interested in the larger story of why we are here. What is this all about, really? Most of my life I have felt out of sync with the larger world around me. I ask questions others don't ask. I see things others don't see. I say things others don't say. I was, and I still am, enamoured by magic and the unseen mystery that surrounds us all knowing that there is something more to this life.

In a basic way, I have always felt an inner call to the healing path, one that was deeply spiritual and connected. I earned the capacity for deep attunement to dynamics through the challenges in my lived experience. I had an awareness and a sensitivity that was a great strength and also a wearying burden that drove me to my room, and to books, for refuge and retreat. As a result, I was compelled to seek wholeness in my own life and I committed my life to working with others to heal.

My path was dotted by a mainline Christian upbringing with occasional visitations from the unseen realms. I remember seeing beings in my bedroom and walking in my backyard touching our trees looking for something I couldn't name—a voice, a sign, a knowing. I would read books about healers and my Bible became the voice that talked to me just when I needed support. I remember the day I stumbled onto Ecclesiastes 3 and read the words, "To everything there is a season and a time and place for every purpose under heaven" and I felt divine wisdom and a powerful presence surrounding me.

I had much to encounter within me and so my years of personal healing and psychological training helped me to face and overcome my own pain while walking hour after hour with determined and faithful clients over the last 25 years. I made it my quest to learn various models of healing, even when I was questioned by my colleagues, that honored experiential, body-based treatments that bypassed the mind and opened paths for change that danced in the space of transformation.

During all of this, I was living an ordinary life— raising a family, serving as a professor of counseling, training others in a specialized model of couple treatment, and walking with couples and individuals in the best way I knew how. I went to church and prayed, finding all of my systems and strategies falling flat as something else began to rise. For, there was a deep nagging within me that wouldn't go away. For all of my training and know-how, I was being led to unlearn and release more deeply into the unknowns that my life was delivering to me.

I found myself taking risks that placed me outside of the

orthodoxy of the faith that had held me—had delivered me at 18—from a deep form of loneliness. My curiosity compelled me to try things at the edge, like energy sessions and birth chart readings, to provide some form of guidance for these nagging questions. I found Jungian Depth Psychology more and more helpful as I entered the realm of symbol and took seriously the landscape of the dream. And, my well-crafted life started to unravel as my ordered house of cards began to fall. I remember one moment in particular when I was perched over a figurative cliff. It was a simple family meal when I heard the question that was pressing on me. What if there is more to this life than what I see and have created? I knew that if I didn't jump, I would die, literally, and yet I was sure that another form of death awaited me if I vaulted into the empty space below. I could no longer live the life I had created and yet it felt like death to take that first step into the unknown.

The awakening sparks that you will learn about were dotted throughout my life, but it was as if they collected themselves together over a few years and they demanded my response. With fear and trepidation I became trained in Integrative Energetic Medicine and began exploring the subtle realms allowing the guidance that I had known in my heart to become my guide through it all. I could write a whole book on the path of opening that opened me and the fortuitous and at times circuitous path that walked me. No one would have known from the outside, but my well formed life began to dismantle and I could no longer do what I had done for the last 25 years of my life—no matter how good it looked to the observer.

The path I walked was one of release, into the burning fires that destroyed what was not of my soul and purified what was. I said a deep yes to this path and even in the midst of the struggle I felt more at home than I ever had.

I now realize that I had been out of sync with the world

specifically because the world was not my true home. For all of those years of striving, I now rest more fully in the ordinary simplicity that is life. I walk the woods— listening from within to the spaces in between— and I offer a place for people to meet this truth within themselves. I do less than I've ever done— simplifying, thinking less, and allowing more while I watch in awe how life is guiding me and those around me in the true path of restoration.

It's funny, as I look back now at all of the things I was frightened to lose, that I was sure would destroy me if I opened up and allowed, they aren't even there. What my mind created as form—jobs, people, situations, circumstances—that were necessary for my well-being and existence are like smoke to me now. Not one of them was necessary, or in many cases really wanted, and most of the people I was sure would call me crazy are themselves now beginning to awaken and return home.

I feel honored and grateful for being guided home, for the pain and angst that compelled me for so many years is no longer within me and things just simply are as they are. I've known for many years that my soul call is to help people "remember who they are."

To awaken is to position yourself within the place of the soul so that you can listen from within, from what is true about who and what you are. My soul is content for now I can walk more lightly upon the earth and see with eyes of true joy the beauty of the world that surrounds us all.

Made in the USA
Middletown, DE
27 January 2022